Assessing the Academic Networked Environment: Strategies and Options

February 1996

Charles R. McClure   •   **Cynthia L. Lopata**

ISBN: 0-918006-28-7

Coalition for Networked Information
21 Dupont Circle, Suite 800
Washington, D.C. 20036
202-296-5098 (phone)
202-872-0884 (fax)
http://www.cni.org/CNI.homepage.html (URL)

Order Information: pubs@cni.org

Price $15

*The paper used in this publication meets the minimum requirements of American National Standard for Information
Sciences — Permanence of Paper for Printed Library Materials, ANSI Z39.50-199X.*

Published by the Association of Research Libraries for the Coalition for Networked Information.

PREFACE

If you are reading this then you have noticed an important and relatively recent shift in what higher education talks about when it talks about networks. And, you want help in making this shift in your own approach to the academic networked environment, perhaps in that of your entire institution as well. Almost everyone in higher education now looks to networks and networked resources and services when formulating strategies for addressing the enduring missions of the life of the mind: learning, teaching, research, and community service. But, are we seeing the same things? Are those things the ones we should be seeing? Even more important, are they real, or are they illusions or even projections of what we expect or want to see?

These are the questions posed by the new conversation about networking in higher education. They go to "value" more than they go to "vision." They address impacts, intended and unintended, beneficial and harmful. And, they call out and unintended, beneficial and harmful. And, they call out for new thinking about assessment and evaluation.

This manual is dedicated to answering these sorts of questions. In it McClure and Lopata provide an insightful and courageous treatment of what proved to be a very difficult conceptual and methodological challenge. Along the way they overcame the fact that most of us have precious little *trustworthy* experience with what works and doesn't work in the academic networked environment. And, they also overcame the fact that many of us still unfailingly choose to do something new rather than capturing and analyzing the lessons of what we are already doing. Both of these are understandable, forgivable features of the contemporary networking landscape, especially in the face of the mind-boggling rate of technological and other change. But we need to move beyond them if we are to ensure the future of higher education, let alone to preserve its past. With this manual McClure and Lopata give us a rich and varied set of tools for doing precisely this. We can now begin the hard, long-term work of carefully gauging the extent of our progress into the academic networked environment and reckoning how far we still have to go.

McClure and Lopata recommend this manual to us as the "beta version" of a work in an ongoing process of "testing, refinement, and re-writing." They emphasize that it provides strategies and options that should be considered when assessing the networked environment," and that it is definitely not a cookbook for evaluation. They anticipate that this manual will be revised and expanded in light of a gathering tide of experience with it at a growing number of institutions of higher education.

The Coalition for Networked Information is eager to make good on their expectation. As McClure and Lopata graciously acknowledge, the Coalition has supported the important work that spawned this manual from its very beginning. We are now preparing to issue a "call for statements of interest and experience" from institutions and organizations that are able and willing to work together to devise and then implement a common assessment strategy based upon this manual. This new Coalition initiative will yield invaluable information on the actual impacts of networking on higher education as well as interpretations of and improvements to this manual. We will expand the circle of institutions involved in this effort as quickly as it is prudently possible to do so.

Higher education owes a tremendous debt to McClure and Lopata for bringing their work to such an comendable conclusion. It is a debt best repaid by putting this manual to work not only to the benefit of the future of higher education networking but to the benefit of the future of higher education itself. We hear you Chuck and Cynthia, loud and clear. Thanks!

Paul Evan Peters
Executive Director
Coalition for Networked Information
<paul@cni.org>

February 21, 1996

Acknolwedge-ments

A number of individuals and organizations contributed their time and expertise to this project. Throughout the study graduate students at Syracuse University, School of Information Studies contributed much work to both the project and the manual. These students include Anne Diekma, Bill Gibbons, Bill Boroson, Jean Van Doren, Kristin Eschenfelder, Denise Masters, Makiko Miwa, Diane Sotak, and Claire Urfels. The project could not have been completed without their involvement and commitment.

The manual is a product of a study funded by the U.S. Department of Education through the Higher Education Act, College Library Technology and Co-operation Grants, Research and Demonstration Program, Grant No. R197D40019-94A. We acknowledge the support from this grant which made possible the development of this manual.

We also want to acknowledge the assistance and time provided by the three academic institutions that participated in the site visits and field testing of some aspects of the manual. In each instance, the individuals at these sites assisted the study team by identifying key issues related to the measurement of networked services and activities, offered insights as to how assessments might be better accomplished, and suggested strategies that might improve the means by which networked services could be provided more effectively. We greatly appreciate the contributions of these individuals.

Throughout the study, numerous individuals served as reviewers or otherwise critiqued drafts of the manual. These reviewers met with the study team at various professional conferences, provided comments and suggestions, or served on the study team's Expert Panel. The reviews, suggestions, and comments from these individuals were invaluable as a means for obtaining feedback from people in the field who would actually use the manual. Moreover, their suggestions greatly strengthened specific assessment techniques described in the manual.

We also want to acknowledge the assistance of a number of individuals here at Syracuse University in Computing and Media Services who met with the study team, answered numerous questions regarding evaluation techniques, and offered good ideas and strategies for specific assessment strategies. The interest, involvement, and support from these individuals were important ingredients for completing the project.

A special note of thanks also goes to Patricia Brennan for her copy editing of the manual and to Beth Mahoney for the final production of the manual.

The Coalition for Networked Information (CNI) through Paul Evan Peters and Joan Lippincott deserves a special note of thanks. Their support for helping to organize reviewer meetings, handling a range of logistical matters related to these meetings, and providing moral support throughout the project are greatly appreciated. The assistance of CNI for publishing and disseminating this manual as well as making an electronic version of the manual available over the net are also greatly appreciated.

Charles R. McClure <cmcclure@mailbox.syr.edu>
Cynthia Lopata <cllopata@mailbox.syr.edu>

February 15, 1996

Table of Contents

PART I:

INTRODUCTION

The idea of the "academic networked environment" encompasses a range of campus electronic networked activities and services. Minimally, the academic networked environment includes information and media services, products, hardware and software, and resources which are received by campus users via electronic networks. In this environment, many information services are provided by local, regional, and national networks. Locally developed information services (i.e., from the library, computing services, administration, individuals, or academic departments) may comprise the majority of the academic networked environments.

Despite the fact that many institutions of higher education have built significant networks and have connected to the Internet as part of the evolving National Information Infrastructure (NII), there is little knowledge of how such connectivity has affected the academic institution. To maintain fiscal responsibility, as well as a commitment to providing quality services to users, institutions may wish to address the following key questions:

- What is the volume and type of networking taking place on a particular academic campus?

- Who are the users that access the academic network and what types of services do they utilize?

- How much do the various types of network activities and services cost?

- How has access to and use of networked information resources and services affected teaching, research, learning, service, and other aspects of traditional academic life?

To date, research offers little practical guidance to assess the impact of networking on traditional areas of academic institutional performance such as teaching, research, and service (McClure and Lopata, 1995). Researchers and academic administrators are just beginning to develop measures related to network use that target specific audiences within the institution such as faculty, administrators, librarians, students, and staff.

There is a growing interest in identifying and measuring the impacts of networks on campus. Answers to questions such as "does the campus network improve the productivity of faculty?" or "is networking worth the cost?" are impossible to answer without first defining and calculating some basic measurement techniques. But answers to these questions will first require data about who uses the network, what the network is used for, and what costs are associated with developing and maintaining the network.

While many academic institutions are eager to find answers to questions concerning the impacts of networking, most have yet to obtain data that describe the more basic networking services and activities. This manual proposes a variety of basic assessment techniques with which to begin an evaluation of networking on any given campus.

Indeed, developing measures to assess *impacts* of networking has proven to be a challenging endeavor because of the lack of even basic measures that describe and assess the academic networked environment. Methods for simply counting types of users and their network activities require the resolution of a range of issues and policies which many campuses have yet to address. Typically, before impact measures can be developed, basic measures that describe the extensiveness, efficiency, and effectiveness of academic networking must be created. The results from these measures can serve as a foundation for the creation of impact measures.

One organization, CAUSE, has begun to stress the importance of ongoing evaluation of networked services with their publication of two useful tools, *Self-Assessment for Campus Information Technology Services* (Fleit, 1994), and *Evaluation Guidelines for Institutional Information Resources* (HEIRAlliance, 1995). These tools can be found in Appendix A. Those in the process of assessing the academic networked environment can incorporate the self-assessment techniques provided in these materials with the performance measures and other techniques described here. These approaches are mutually supportive and can be beneficial for those engaged in an ongoing process of assessment.

Background on the Development of this Manual

This manual results from a larger study, "Assessing the Academic Networked Environment," which was conducted from October, 1994 through December, 1995. The authors of this manual were also the co-principal investigators for the study. The purpose of this study was to develop a model of the academic networked environment and propose techniques to assess the academic networked environment.

The following research questions guided the investigation:

- What information technologies and services comprise networked information, and to what degree are these similar across various academic institutions?

- Who are the "users" of networked information within the academic setting and how might we develop a typology of such users?

- What are the organizational structures used in academic institutions to provide networked information services?

- What are the key factors that appear to affect the overall success of the networked environment in an academic setting?

- What assessment techniques and specific measures can be developed to assess the academic networked environment?

An exploratory, qualitative data collection approach combined multiple data collection techniques such as focus groups, small group interviews, site visits, analysis of academic computing strategic plans, review by experts and expert panels, and literature review.

Findings from the study are presented in the final report (Lopata and McClure, 1996). Key issues, however, that emerged from this research include:

- An adequate network infrastructure is believed to be essential to attract and retain high quality faculty and students.

- There are no generally accepted measures for use in evaluating network facilities and services.

- Networks are becoming increasingly complex and distributed and therefore more difficult to support and maintain.

- Existing technologies and information services are lagging behind user demand.

- The absence of good measures of teaching, research, and learning prior to networking will make it difficult to assess networking's impacts.

- There are numerous barriers that limit the degree to which academic institutions engage in a regular ongoing program of network evaluation and assessment.

- Elements of the academic networked environment which may be consistent across institutions include: electronic mail, campus-wide information systems, and listservs; constituent groups, including administrators, staff, faculty, students, and the community; and a technological support structure.

Other issues and findings from the study are detailed in the final report. Suffice to say here, however, that material included in this manual is based on work performed in the original study. Overall, the findings suggested that academic institutions needed a concise guide to evaluating the campus network that employed a range of assessment techniques.

Objectives of this Manual

This manual is an initial attempt to offer strategies and options for academic institutions to use in collecting information to assess their academic networked environment. While the manual refers to sources of special interest for a given topic, it is not intended to provide a literature review of topics related to assessing academic networking. The manual has the following objectives:

- Describe a range of techniques that assess the academic networked environment.

- Provide procedures for collecting and analyzing the data needed to produce an assessment of the academic networked environment.

- Identify and discuss data collection issues and problems that may be encountered when conducting such assessments.

- Encourage academic institutions to engage in a regular program of ongoing evaluation and assessment of their computing networks.

- Provide a baseline for conducting network assessments as a means for improving academic networked services.

The manual can assist network managers and higher education decision makers with improving the usefulness and quality of their networks and ultimately increasing the satisfaction of network users.

Audience

This manual is targeted to a number of different types of people in the higher education community. University administrators will find the assessment techniques useful as a basis for strategic planning and for determining the degree to which networked services support the larger goals and mission of the institution. Those responsible for the day-to-day management and operation of the campus network will find that the manual helps monitor and fine-tune network support and services; to determine which aspects of the network are working well versus those working less well; and to report to institutional administrators on the overall development of the network.

Users of academic networks will also find this manual of interest. The manual encourages the direct involvement of users in the assessment of academic networking. It provides users with a means to assess the network in terms of the degree to which the network meets *their* needs. In addition, the manual will be of interest to researchers attempting to develop assessment techniques and specific measures for assessing the academic networked environment. The proposed strategies, guidelines, and options can be built upon by other researchers to extend and refine the assessment techniques.

Additionally, the information in this manual can be useful in the accreditation process as accrediting bodies update their criteria for assessing the quality and currency of higher education institutions. A brief review of accreditation standards for postsecondary institutions found that the accrediting bodies are just beginning to develop criteria for information technologies and networks available on campuses. Currently, none of the six regional accrediting bodies for higher education have established a standard that addresses the overall campus technological environment.

All of the accrediting agencies, however, have incorporated, to varying degrees, some criteria for information technology resources within their 'Library and Information' standards. Approaches range from prescriptive to optional standards that address access to technology, available technology training for effective student and faculty use, and incorporation of technology into operations. Accrediting agencies may find the measures and assessment techniques in this manual a helpful beginning point for developing accreditation criteria in this area.

Finally, it should be pointed out that originally the primary institutions targeted to use this manual were Carnegie I and II institutions of higher education. However, the pretesting and review of the manual by a range of individuals in other types of institutions convinced the study team that much of the manual could be applied to other types of academic institutions. Thus, depending on the status of networking at a particular institution, some aspects of the manual will be of greater benefit than others.

Organization of the Manual

The manual consists of five parts. The first part is an introductory overview of the manual. Part II presents guidelines and suggestions for collecting qualitative data that assess the networked environment. This is often an underutilized approach in evaluations of technology, but can provide useful and cost-effective information about the campus network. This section of the manual identifies topics which can be investigated using a number of possible qualitative methods, and it offers suggestions regarding the best ways to use these methods.

Part III presents a set of measures designed to describe the extent to which the network is used, the efficiency and effectiveness of networked information services and activities, and the impact of networking on such traditional areas of academic performance as teaching, learning, and research. Part III of the manual describes six key assessment areas in which quantitative data can be collected:

- Users: the number and types of users and the frequency with which they use the campus network

- Costs: the total and types of financial resources that are expended to operate the academic network

- Network traffic: the amount and types of traffic flowing over the academic network

- Use: the amount and types of uses made of the network

- Services: the applications and services that are made available over the network

- Support: the types of assistance that network administrators make available to the users of the network

Some measures address two or more of these areas but have been organized within the assessment area that they best represent.

Part IV of the manual addresses the importance of user surveys to assess the network. This section also provides sample questions for a network user survey that complements the data collection described in the earlier sections. The objectives of the survey are to obtain a user-based assessment of network services and activities and determine the degree to which users are satisfied with those services. The survey questions are designed to collect data on the following:

- User Demographics: characteristics of user subgroups.

- Campus Computing Network: use of, and satisfaction with, network access and applications.

- Network Support: use of, and satisfaction with, support services such as online help, help desk, workshops, and printed guides.

- Public Computing Facilities: use of, and satisfaction with, network access via on-campus public access computers.

- User Evaluation: specific network problems and benefits identified by users.

Depending on the specific situation, additional topics can be identified for use in the survey.

The manual concludes with a final section, Part V, that summarizes the importance of ongoing assessment, discusses the need for campus administrators to implement assessment techniques, and suggests that future developments in higher education will require increased attention to assessing the network and uses of computing technology.

Defining the Campus Network

Throughout the manual, the authors refer to "the network" or "the campus network." Determining what, exactly constitutes the network or the campus network is an extremely complicated task in itself. Yet, without a clear sense of how best to define these terms, measurement is quite problematic. Each institution using this manual will have to determine for itself how best to define its campus network, that is to determine those components that constitute and support the networked activities and services they are assessing.

There is no easy or straight-forward method to operationalize a definition of the campus network. It may be helpful to think of the network as comprising these components:

- The Technical Infrastructure: the hardware, software, equipment, communication lines, and technical aspects of the network

- Content: the information resources available on the network

- Services: the activities in which users can engage and the services that users may use complete various tasks

- Support: the assistance and support services provided to help users better use the network

- Management: the human resources, governance, planning, and fiscal aspects of the network.

These five basic components suggest the extent to which the campus network can be described and defined.

The manual focuses attention on assessing those aspects of the campus network and not the broader national or global networked environment — although clearly, those national and global aspects of networking will affect the local campus network. Thus, individual institutions may wish to define their campus network in terms of the degree to which *they maintain control over aspects of these five components*. Since those aspects over which the institution can maintain control will vary from campus to campus, each institution will need to define as best it can, what specifically constitutes *its* campus network.

The authors recognize that the definition of the "network" will likely vary from institution to institution, indeed, the definition will need to vary due to factors unique at each institution. Nonetheless, a definition should be developed as it forms the foundation for using this manual.

Performance Measures and Evaluation

Performance measures are a broad managerial tool that encompass measurement of inputs (indicators of the resources essential to provide a service), outputs (indicators of the services resulting from the use of those resources), and impacts (the effect of these outputs on other variables or factors). Performance measures serve a number of useful purposes, but above all they are an essential means to assess the academic networked environment. They can:

- Identify the successful and less successful aspects of the network in light of user needs and institutional goals.

- Provide trend data to assess changes in the network and network services over time.

- Assist decision makers in allocating or reallocating resources and in planning for future network development.

- Assist network managers in justifying expenditures and accounting for those expenditures.

- Monitor network activities and services to detect any changes in activities or the quality of services.

- Determine the degree to which users are satisfied with the network and network services.

- Serve as a first step in benchmarking (identifying best-practice performance, using that performance as a goal, investigating the factors that led to the performance, and then trying to replicate that level of performance).

Simply stated, performance measures ask decision makers to answer the questions: How well is the service or activity doing what its providers claim it should be doing? At what cost? And with what effects?

Although there are a number of ways to categorize measures, one approach is to think of measures as concentrating primarily on one of the following areas:

- Extensiveness: this is a measure of the amount or extent to which the services are provided, for example, the number and types of people using the service.

- Efficiency: this is a measure of the cost or resources required to provide the service, for example, cost per service transaction.

- Effectiveness: an effectiveness measure is one that focuses attention on the degree to which the objectives of the program or service are met.

- Service Quality: such measures are concerned with how well a service or activity is done, e.g., percentage of transactions where users acquire the information they need.

- Impact: an impact measure focuses attention on the benefit or result of the service or activity, e.g., the degree to which using the Internet services empowered the user to resolve other problems or improved his/her quality of life.

- Usefulness: this is a measure of appropriateness, that is, the degree to which the services are useful or appropriate for the individual user, e.g., percentage of services of interest to different types of user audiences.

Measures and assessment strategies offered in this manual cover all of these areas although there is less development of impact measures. But these areas for assessment suggest the importance of considering different types of measures in assessing various aspects of the campus network.

Clearly, performance measures can assist managers in formally evaluating the network. This evaluation involves identifying and collecting data about specific services or activities, establishing criteria to assess their success, and determining the degree to which the service or activity accomplishes stated objectives. Evaluation, however, also reflects *value judgements* on the part of the evaluator regarding the adequacy, appropriateness, and success of a particular service or activity. The evaluation process encourages these value judgments regarding *appropriate* levels or quality of services to be made explicit.

In a broader organizational context, resource allocation, planning, and improving services require measurement and evaluation of networked information services. Without measures that can evaluate particular services, decision makers must rely on intuition and anecdotal information as a basis for assessing the usefulness and value of a particular service. Perhaps most importantly, measurement and evaluation provide users with an opportunity to offer feedback on how well services are meeting their needs.

Developing, operationalizing, and validating a range of performance measures is essential if an academic institution intends to: determine which networked information services are effective; understand the impacts of networking on the educational process; and identify the costs required to build and maintain the network. Without such information, administrators of networked systems and services in the academic setting may be unable to justify, or less equipped to justify, such services and unable to meet user needs.

Assessment in the Distributed Network and Computing Environment

The distributed network and computing environment now in place at most academic institutions is one where many individuals, departments, and other administrative units are involved in the design, administration, and operation of the network and computing services. There is usually some type of central computing and network unit with responsibilities for the entire campus. Increasingly, however, individual departments and units have administrative and operational responsibilities for a range of computing and network services in their particular unit.

The degree to which the academic campus has distributed networking and computing services will, of course, vary from campus to campus. But the current trend appears to be the development of a more distributed networking and computing environment. The implications of this trend on network assessment techniques are significant.

- Oftentimes there is no single person or unit that is "in charge" of networking development and services. Thus, obtaining data about a specific networking service or activity requires the evaluator to work with a number of individuals or units on campus.

- Distributed systems, with different system administrators, and with varying levels of interest in evaluation, may have different types of data that measure very different aspects of the network. Thus, seemingly simple counts such as the number of users of the network may, in fact, be problematic.

- The evaluation techniques and measures that are needed and are appropriate for campus-wide assessment may be different from those needed by an individual department. As a result, some of the measures and data collection techniques suggested in this manual may be appropriate both in a campus-wide context and for an individual department. Other measures, however, may not.

- The distributed computing and networking environment may result in an overlap of services, user confusion regarding which unit is responsible for what service, and a poor understanding of the technical basis of the network. Thus, measures that are dependent on some technical aspect of the network may change, making the measure irrelevant.

In short, the distributed networking and computing environment found on many campuses may complicate the process for ongoing evaluation and performance assessment.

The measures and data collection techniques suggested in this manual are intended, primarily, to be used in a campus-wide context and to provide a broad assessment of networking on the campus as a whole. Nonetheless, many of the measures and techniques can be used by individual units for assessing a particular distributed part of the network. The assessment techniques may also be useful for institutions with multiple campuses. Some modifications may be needed for such use of the techniques in these contexts; assessment, however, of networking campus-wide and of the various parts of the distributed network are *both* important.

Importance of Management Information Systems

Data resulting from assessments may be more effectively collected and used if a management information system (MIS) is in place at the institution. The term MIS is meant to describe a computer-based information system, comprised of a variety of regularly collected management data, that provides decision makers with a range of information that supports the decision making process. Underlying assumptions are that decision makers can identify the information they need for their decision making process, that the data can be obtained and organized, and that decision makers will use the information if it is available.

An effective MIS provides decision makers with accurate and timely information that improves the information base from which decisions are made. Users of this manual may wish to consider creating a MIS to capture, organize, analyze, compare, and report a range of data describing network activities and services. The MIS should support a number of different types of decision making, including:

- Operational Decisions: day-to-day decision making.

- Strategic Planning Decisions: determining appropriate objectives and assessing the degree to which those objectives were accomplished.

- "What if" Questions: if we increase expenditures on a particular service, what would the impact be on other services?

- Exceptions: access to a particular database on the campus wide information system increased drastically last month, why?

- Resource Control: ensuring that resources are expended on appropriate activities or items.

An effective MIS also supplies decision makers with accurate and timely information in both standardized and customized formats — depending on the needs of the user.

Unfortunately, many academic institutions have yet to formalize some type of MIS for their network and thus are unable to:

- Comprehensively capture, organize, analyze, and report information that describes network activities and services, network-related costs and expenditures, users of the network, and other institutional information related to the network

- Identify and respond to network service strengths and weaknesses or the needs of network users

- Demonstrate the overall effectiveness and efficiency of the network, track various service or use trends, and report such information on a timely basis

- Simplify and standardize network data gathering and reporting procedures across the institution

- Monitor ongoing network activities and project network costs effectively.

Perhaps most importantly, institutions without some type of MIS are unable to determine which specific types of data are most important for collection and analysis. Thus, data collection activities to monitor and assess the network are haphazard, uncoordinated, and likely to vary across the institution depending on who collects the data.

The manual does not provide a tutorial on how to develop a MIS. A number of useful sources are available that provide information regarding the development of an MIS (e.g., Wetherbe, 1993). Academic institutions, however, that use the performance measures and other data collection techniques suggested in this manual should also consider developing a MIS to maintain and organize the data that are collected. A formal approach for collecting and managing network information will enhance the usefulness of the performance measures

and will help to improve, significantly, the overall ongoing program to assess and improve the campus network.

Integrating Evaluation into the Planning Process

It is important to stress that ongoing evaluation is a vital source of information for an institution's planning process. Typically the needs assessment activities within a planning process include a review and assessment of the network which assists decision makers in determining the degree to which objectives have been accomplished. Developing goals and objectives with no follow-up effort to determine how well those objectives were actually accomplished significantly reduces the overall value of both planning and the use of assessment techniques.

Institutional plans for information technology and networked information services take on increased importance given the rapidly changing environment in which such services are offered. In developing institutional plans for networked information services an assessment of the existing quality and range of services is essential—this manual can assist planners by offering guidelines for conducting such assessments. Typically, such assessment information then provides input into the development of institutional goals and objectives at the department or unit level.

When planning networked information services in an academic environment, there are likely to be a number of departments and units that should be involved in the process. Given the distributed context in which networked information services typically are delivered, coordination and participation among these various units is essential. In addition, careful thought should be given to identifying and linking appropriate performance indicators to the agreed upon objectives. Administrators, then, can determine the degree to which the objectives were, in fact, accomplished.

The manual does not describe planning approaches for campus computing and networking. Whatever the approach chosen by a particular institution, evaluation and use of measures should be an important component of that planning process. Johnson, Rush, and Coopers & Lybrand (1995) offer a useful introduction to planning and financial strategies in higher education.

Using the Manual

The strategies and options offered in this manual were derived from a research effort that obtained assessments and input from a number of site visits and interviews with individuals knowledgeable about academic computing and networking. A key finding from this work is the limited knowledge and minimal use of assessment techniques in the academic networked environment. Participants in the study noted the importance of using a range of assessment techniques — although most did not, in fact, use such techniques. Another finding is that the complexity of the academic networked environment imposes some limitations on the degree to which measures of this environment can be developed.

Non-comparability Across Institutions

Although the manual describes general procedures for collecting data and producing measures, the resulting measures are unlikely to be comparable across different institutions of higher education. The networking infrastructure and the manner in which data travel in different institutions vary considerably. Furthermore, different institutions may use different definitions for key terms, e.g., network user, information technology expenditures, etc. While these concerns will not hinder the use of these measures in one particular institution, they will limit the degree to which results can be compared across institutions.

Developing Assessment Policies and Procedures

To a certain extent, users of the manual may have to develop policies and define data collection activities within a range of organizational and network constraints. Indeed, some institutions may not currently have the capacity to collect the data needed for some of these performance measures. In such instances, the academic institution will need to first determine how best the data can be collected, develop a system or approach for collecting and analyzing that data, and develop policies that formalize a management information system to insure that the data continue to be collected in a regular and standardized fashion. While such efforts are essential, they are beyond the scope of this manual.

During the course of this research project, participants revealed a number of different views and experiences regarding the types of assessment techniques and measures that would be most useful given an institution's particular situation. The approach taken in this manual is to identify and describe a number of different assessment techniques and measures. Depending on the nature of the network, the administrative concerns regarding that network, and networking/institutional goals and objectives, some of the following assessment techniques and measures may be more useful for some institutions than others.

Interpreting Results

The results from the use of these assessment techniques and measures have greater meaning when considered in the broader context of:

- Institutional and networking goals and objectives at a particular institution.

- Other assessment information describing institutional activities, services, and participants.

- Various time periods and the amount of change in a particular measure over time.

- The amount of resources and their allocation to the network infrastructure and services.

- Comparison of assessment techniques and results to other *similar* institutions.

- Factors related to a particular institution, its networking configuration, or other variables unique to that institution.

In short, value judgments as to whether a score on a particular measure is "good" or "bad" are dependent on a range of other factors. Interpretation of performance measure scores should be done in consideration of other organizational and institutional factors.

The accuracy of the resulting assessment techniques and measures is directly related to the quality of the data collected, the use of standardized procedures, and the development of institutional policies that define these data collection activities. In a sense, these assessment techniques might be best seen as initial estimates of the extensiveness, efficiency, effectiveness, or impact of a service or activity rather than a precise measure of that particular service or activity. As institutions maintain longitudinal data and gain experience in collecting data and producing such measures, the quality of the assessments will improve.

Confidentiality and Internal Data Collection Procedures

The assumption throughout the various data collection activities suggested in this manual is that in those instances where data might be linked to individuals, only aggregates and summaries would be reported. Confidentiality of responses gathered via surveys or other data collection techniques should be insured. Moreover, individual institutions may have policies and procedures to be followed for collecting data on human subjects or to conduct campus-wide surveys. Users of the manual may wish to review such institutional procedures and policies related to data collection and assessment prior to attempting the assessment techniques described here.

Level of Effort

Given the limited resources available to most institutions, campus administrators may wish to pick and chose the assessment techniques they wish to use. They may wish, for example to take a specific area, such as the help desk, and use a quantitative measure as well as survey and anecdotal information to assess the quality of the service the help desk offers. In addition to being selective about the techniques to use, some institutions have "outsourced" networking assessments by contracting with other individuals or firms to conduct an assessment.

The suggested measures, user survey, and the qualitative approaches can all be modified to meet the specific needs and context of each institution.

For example, institutions may want to select some questions from the survey, modify other questions, and add questions of local institutional interest and importance. Institutions should select carefully the measurement approaches that are most feasible and most likely to have the greatest pay-off. Users of the manual are encouraged to think of the manual as a sourcebook for selecting appropriate measures and approaches rather than a guide to be followed step by step.

Encouraging Network Assessment

Finally, it should be emphasized that the manual does not intend to offer detailed procedures to be used for network assessment; *it is not a cookbook for evaluation techniques*. Rather, the manual provides strategies and options that should be considered when assessing the networked environment. At its best, the manual should stimulate evaluators to consider how best to implement the assessment techniques described, how to resolve measurement issues that will be raised during the assessment process, and how to implement a regular program of ongoing assessment.

The manual will be successful if it (1) encourages campus and networking officials to experiment with some of the assessment techniques described herein, (2) provides additional information and insight about how such assessments can be done more effectively, (3) moves evaluation research concepts and procedures forward in this area, (4) assists campus decision makers to design and plan more effective networked environments, and (5) promotes the incorporation of user assessments and views on how the network should evolve.

PART II:

COLLECTING AND USING QUALITATIVE DATA

Qualitative data are data that describe, explain, and characterize the subject of investigation using words rather than numbers. Quantitative data collection and analysis techniques may be used, for example, to determine *how often*, on average, network users connect to the network, while qualitative data collection and analysis techniques may be used to *characterize* their use of the network in terms of *what* they do on the network, *how* they do it, and *why* they use the network.

Qualitative techniques are especially appropriate for use in situations where the research problem and the research setting are *not* well understood. When the problem and setting *are* well understood, the investigator can obtain information to develop survey questions and quantitative measures. When it is not clear what questions should be asked or what should be measured, a qualitative approach will be more useful.

Evaluation of academic networking is in the very early stages. Thus qualitative techniques will be especially useful in developing an understanding of the users of networks as well as the benefits and problems associated with network use. A key advantage to using qualitative data collection techniques is that participants often are interviewed and observed in their natural settings. Thus, they can more conveniently participate, they may be able to more accurately answer questions about their settings, and the researcher gets a firsthand look at the settings as the participants describe them.

Qualitative approaches allow the participants to raise topics and issues which the evaluator did not anticipate and which might be critical to the investigation. They also allow participants to express their feelings and offer their perspectives in their own words. Often participants will provide examples or anecdotes that illustrate a particular point-of-view. These anecdotes can be very powerful and persuasive when evaluators are reporting findings. This is in direct contrast to a survey in which respondents may answer only the questions which are included on the survey and, when the questions are close-ended, respondents must select an answer from a list of possible answers. In sum, the strength of qualitative research is that it is best for exploratory and descriptive analyses which stress the importance of context, setting, and subjects' frames of reference (Marshall & Rossman, 1994).

While either qualitative or quantitative methods can be used alone to assess academic networking, a more powerful approach is to combine qualitative and quantitative methods. A well designed evaluation of a network is likely to include both types of research methods. Quantitative research techniques and data collection provides a sound basis for statistical projection. Qualitative research findings should not be used to generalize to populations that are presumed to be similar to the one under study.

Overview of Qualitative Techniques

A complete discussion of qualitative evaluation research designs and social science research methods is beyond the scope of this manual. Specific information on these topics can be found in a number of useful texts, including Rossi and Freeman (1993), Babbie (1992), Denzin and Lincoln (1994), and Marshall and Rossman (1994). This section highlights a number of data collection techniques useful in developing qualitative evaluations of institutional networks. Specifics for using these techniques can be found in textbooks listed above or in other research methods texts. The selection of one or more of these techniques will be a function of the institutional resources available for data collection and analysis as well as the type of data and results desired. Potential users of these techniques are advised to consult trained individuals at their institutions for guidance and assistance.

Network Benchmarking

Benchmarking is a business measurement strategy which Terplan (1995) defines as the "... in-depth comparison of network management functions and instruments of two or more companies in order to establish quantifiable indicators of network management efficiency" (p. back cover). It can be used to expose the discrepancies between measures of one's own network performance and management and measures of an entire industry. Comparisons can be made against industry averages or best practices. For example, Charles Bowsher, Comptroller General of the United States, proposed a plan to reengineer various offices of the U.S. federal government. In his proposal, Bowsher (1994) recommends benchmarking government information management practices against leading organizations selected according to objective data or recognized criteria.

The first step in benchmarking is identifying what activities or processes need to be benchmarked. Terplan (1995) provides an exhaustive list of possible benchmarking indicators including generic indicators, organizational indicators, specific network management process indicators, and cost indicators. Boxwell (1994) advises his readers to choose activities that explicitly increase the organization's value.

The second step involves identifying comparative organizations. Ideally, a network analyst wants to know how the organization is performing compared to the industry average as well as compared to the organization's strongest competitor.

The third step consists of collecting the benchmarking data. Terplan (1995) offers a comprehensive assessment guide in which he suggests using his preliminary questionnaire to assess company background, applications, transmission facilities, networking equipment, personnel, costs, and basic network management. A more probing on-site interview questionnaire is then recommended to assess, "... investments and organizational structure; networking management functions and problems; the implementation of processes, protocols, and instruments; and the direction of network management" (p. 81). A final questionnaire, which is even more in-depth, is used for analyzing single network management processes and functions. These three questionnaires are then combined with observations of the client contact point, operations, and shift takeover. Lastly, Terplan recommends a comprehensive analysis of the aforementioned indicators for network management.

Data analysis is the fourth step in benchmarking. The quantitative data collected in step three are consolidated and entered into a statistical software package (e.g., SPSS, SAS, etc.). Specific analytical procedures will depend on the indicators themselves. Findings are then compared with findings from organizations identified in Step two. Recommendations to network managers are developed based on this interpretation of the data.

Although benchmarking is an effective measurement technique to help an information systems department become aware of its position as compared to industry standards, it is not without problems. Requirements for effective benchmarking include: researchers with the appropriate skills, training, and experience; and an adequate, representative sample of organizations from the appropriate industry. These requirements may be difficult to meet in the higher education field where a "culture" of ongoing evaluation is virtually nonexistent. Until more academic institutions participate regularly in rigorous benchmarking practices, this technique will be difficult to implement.

Focus Groups

This qualitative data collection technique is extremely valuable for obtaining naturalistic insights into how individuals perceive networks and network impacts (Morgan, 1993). With this technique, the evaluator identifies a particular group of individuals (usually 5-11 people) that meet certain criteria (e.g., members of the academic community). The individuals (who typically do not know each other) are brought together to discuss aspects of the topic at hand. The session typically lasts one to two hours, and is conducted in a conference room setting, with a moderator and a note-taker from the study team participating in the session (Krueger, 1994).

A focus group session differs from a group interview in that participants in a focus group are encouraged to make contributions to the discussion beyond simply answering the moderator's questions. The moderator should have a short list of questions to ask during the session, but these questions should be broad. And the moderator should allow participants to bring up related issues. This approach encourages users to share their perspectives, provides data based on the topics that users believe are most important, and allows the data collection to inform the evaluator about additional topics that might need attention but which otherwise would not have been identified.

Critical Incident Technique

To better understand users' perspectives, sometimes it is helpful to have users describe *specific* recent experiences or incidents related to the topic of the investigation. For example, the investigator might be especially interested in the users' experiences accessing class information via the network. The investigator can ask the users to recall and describe their most recent or memorable uses of the network for this purpose. This technique is likely to provide more details about their use of the network

than if the moderator were to ask the users to simply discuss their use of the network to access class information.

The critical incident technique may be used in an interview or in a survey. Once the respondent describes a specific experience or incident, the investigator may probe (in an interview) or ask a standard list of exploratory questions (in a survey). In an interview, the evaluator has much greater flexibility in probing and following up on specific experiences or incidents than in a survey. The critical incident technique is an excellent approach for focusing a user's attention on a particular type of experience or incident and is useful for capturing the rich details of the experience or incident.

User Activity Logs

Another very useful approach is to have users maintain logs that describe: (1) the nature of their experiences regarding some related network activity, (2) the amount of time spent on that particular activity, and (3) the user's assessment of the usefulness or success of that particular activity. A user activity log can be designed to collect information on a range of network activities or it might focus on a particular one of special interest to the evaluator.

It is important that the participants maintaining the logs have a high degree of commitment and are provided with some rewards for engaging in this time-consuming data collection activity. Variations among individuals in their commitment and performance in maintaining the logs will have a negative effect on the results and may introduce bias to the data. Also, it is advisable to recruit a larger sample than necessary, in case some participants fail to complete the logs. Examples of user logs can be found in Doty, Bishop, and McClure (1992).

Typically, the evaluator will identify specific individuals to create and maintain the user logs over some period of time. The users may be segmented to obtain data from specific user types, e.g., novice users versus experienced users. And, depending on the nature of the study, the specific types of information to be collected in the logs may vary. User logs tend to be more useful if maintained over an extended time period, e.g., a month, so that patterns in use may be more easily identified by the evaluator. User logs are especially valuable in that they mirror actual behavior at the point when it occurs rather than the users' recollections of that behavior.

Network-based Data Collection

Another approach to obtaining evaluative information about users and networks is to use the network itself to interact with users and collect data. The evaluator can establish and moderate an online conference on the network about a particular topic and invite selected individuals to participate. Participants are informed that the online discussion will be used as data for the evaluation study. The moderator can play virtually no role in the conference, or he/she can take a very active role. The moderator may refrain from commenting online or may direct the discussion to certain topics and solicit opinions from individuals. The conference may be conducted during a pre-set period of time, or may continue for weeks or months, with participants contributing comments at their convenience.

An advantage of this data collection technique is that it allows participants' views to evolve and inform others as the conference proceeds. Software is available that organizes the conference into particular topics, permits individuals to send messages to one or more members of the conference, and otherwise manages the operation of the conference.

A related technique is to use the network as a means of administering a survey. For example, someone might put a short questionnaire on a newsgroup or listserv and ask for responses (to the evaluator and not the newsgroup or list). One benefit from this approach is that responses are already in electronic format. This technique, while easy to do, has a number of possible problems. First, the evaluator has no control over who will respond. Because of this, the responses may come from individuals who have a vested interest in the topic, thus biasing the sample. Second, many newsgroup and listserv subscribers object to the abundance of messages they receive and may discard electronic surveys or be annoyed at receiving them. Response rates may be so low as to invalidate the results obtained.

Interviews

One of the old standbys for data collection is an interview. Interviews can be done with individuals or with groups. The questions to be posed in the in-

terviews can range from unstructured (little predetermination of topics to be covered) to highly structured (complete determination of the topics to be covered). The success of this technique is largely dependent on the interviewer's skills. Goldman and McDonald (1987) offer a training guide for group interviews. Interviews have the advantage of allowing the evaluator to probe topics, which cannot be done in surveys. They have the disadvantage of requiring considerable time in organizing, conducting, and transcribing the interviews, as well as analyzing the data.

Group Process Surveys

A group process survey is a combination of a survey and an interview. With this technique, the evaluator selects a particular set of participants to examine a topic or an issue. In preparation for the meeting, the evaluator develops a set of discussion topics that are handed out to participants. During the one- to two-hour meeting, the group discusses a particular topic and each participant writes his/her view of the topic on the handout. The moderator can ask that participants write their thoughts on the topic as the discussion is in progress, after the discussion occurs and before moving on to the next topic, or both before and after the actual discussion.

There are a number of advantages to using this technique. First, and perhaps most importantly, the participants write, in their own words, their views on the topic being discussed so that the moderator does not have to reconstruct their comments from his/her notes at a later time. Second, this approach allows participants to be informed by the discussion and modify their views during the discussion. Finally, this technique usually results in a 100% response rate—which rarely occurs with surveys, where people may skip questions, or group discussions, where some people may be unwilling to speak and others may dominate the conversations. A disadvantage is that participants may miss parts of the conversations when they are writing their views.

Site Visits

Site visits are similar to the case study approach (Yin, 1994) except that site visits are not likely to be as time consuming, are more informal, and can be less detailed. Generally, case studies have some longitudinal dimension to them since they are conducted over a period to time. A site visit generally is planned to obtain first-hand information from tours of specific facilities and services, interviews with individuals or groups, or observations of specific activities at the site. In addition, the site visit can be used to obtain reports, brochures, and examples of products or services made available at the site. An interesting aspect of site visits is the potential to directly compare and contrast different types of data collection techniques from different sources within the same site on the same topic.

With site visits, it is not always possible to predict in advance the range of data collection activities in which the researcher might engage. Clearly, some of the data collection strategies can, and should, be planned in advance of the site visit, i.e., scheduling interview times, tours, etc. Additional data collection opportunities, however, may arise as the site visit progresses. Indeed, the evaluator should be extremely conscious of opportunities to meet with individuals or groups that, perhaps, he/she could not have know about until the site visit occurred. One major benefit of site visits is the opportunity to obtain first-hand information about users or activities in a particular setting. Another benefit is the ability to evolve the data collection strategies on site, depending on the topics the evaluator determines are important to probe for obtaining additional information.

Scenario Development

An interesting, but underutilized data collection technique is scenario development. This can be done either as a group or an individual process. The basic idea with this approach is to have participants discuss "what if..." types of questions and construct scenarios, or likely series of events, that would need to occur if a particular vision or goal is to be accomplished. Scenario development is an especially useful technique for having participants consider possible future events, speculate about what key assumptions may drive the development of future events, and suggest the necessary elements for success in a particular scenario.

There are a number of methods for using scenario development as a successful data collection technique (Amara and Lipinski, 1983). One approach is to first carefully define the nature of the scenario to be explored, develop a one-page written description of an example scenario to use with the group (mak-

ing sure it is pre-tested and revised before use), and identify appropriate topics and questions that need to be explored. For example, the scenario might be that a wealthy alumna gives the school money to install fiber optic cable to every desktop, allowing for individual use of immense amounts of bandwidth. Given that scenario, a number of discussion questions might be used with a group: e.g., what new services would become available, how would the new resources affect the way students prepare for classes, and so forth.

The views of group participants when discussing the implications and assumptions for a scenario can provide very useful insights into what users think might, or should, happen in the future. From the evaluator's point of view, these insights can be used to identify issues and policies that might be needed to deal with the issues. Researchers must be careful to choose the appropriate individuals to participate in scenario development. Some training may be necessary for the moderator.

Observations

Observations of users, in a range of situations, or in the use of various services/equipment, are useful in constructing a user perspective. Information gathered through observations can be used to describe users' activities in terms of what they do, how they do it, how long they spend doing it, and problems they encounter.

Observation can be either obtrusive (i.e., the user knows that he/she is being observed) or unobtrusive (i.e., the user is unaware that he/she is being observed). There are trade-offs, in terms of data quality and ease of collection, and ethical issues to consider in deciding which of these two approaches to take (Hernon & McClure, 1986).

A well developed data collection form is essential when doing observations. The evaluator must be able to easily and quickly summarize the activities observed, the length of time in which the user was engaged in that activity, and any comments the evaluator might have at the time of the observation. Also, it may be desirable to use more than one evaluator to observe an activity in order to increase the objectivity of the data. There are a number of useful texts that provide guidance for conducting observations (Epstein & Tripoldi, 1977, pp. 42-54).

Strengths and Weaknesses of Techniques

It is difficult to compare strengths and weaknesses of these techniques. However, there are a number of criteria that may be used in selecting an appropriate technique or group of techniques for use in addressing a specific research question in a designated setting. These include:

- The degree to which the method can provide the appropriate data. For example, if you want to find out why network users are choosing to spend their time in certain ways, interviews might be more appropriate than activity logs. If you want to find out how much time they're spending on various activities, activity logs might be more appropriate.

- The amount of time required to collect and analyze the data. For instance, interview transcripts may be more time-consuming to analyze than activity logs.

- Costs associated with collecting and analyzing the data. This may include: the cost to users who may be collecting the data for the researchers; the cost of outside agents who may be required for specialized tasks like data entry or statistical analysis.

- Requirements for training in the method. This applies to training for researchers as well as for users who may be asked to collect and analyze data, e.g., if they are maintaining user activity logs.

- Degree to which users are required to be involved in the process. Some methods, such as focus groups, require a very limited commitment of time, perhaps a few hours, for those participating. Other methods, such as site visits, may require extensive preparation at the site and involvement with the researchers over a period of days.

- Level of commitment required of participants. Individuals who are required to collect and record data over a long period of time must be highly committed to collecting and recording this data accurately, completely, and consistently. The level of commitment expected of an interviewee is less than that expected of an individual who is maintaining an activity log.

- Degree to which a representation of the entire community is required by the researcher. Interviews with selected individuals may not adequately reflect the range of perspectives in the community that can be captured in a group process survey.

Some of the criteria listed above will be more important than others, depending on the goals of the research and the setting in which the research is being done.

Key Networking Topics and Issues

This section contains a series of suggested topics and issues that may be suitable for investigation via qualitative assessment techniques. The topics and issues identified below may relate to a number of networking applications. For purposes of presentation, however, they are included under the headers for which they appear to have primary importance. These topics can be used with a number of techniques described earlier in this section. For example, a critical incident technique could be employed asking the respondent to recall and describe a situation when the network significantly improved teaching.

The topics and issues listed below are not comprehensive. Rather, they suggest possible topics that lend themselves to assessment via a qualitative approach. Those using the manual will want to add topics and refine those listed here.

Network and Teaching

1. Has the network changed the way you teach (Faculty perception)? If yes, how? Relevant network applications and functions might include:

- Listservs
- Newsgroups
- Web pages
- Software packages
- Telnet sessions to remote computers

2. Has the network improved or harmed the quality of teaching (Faculty and student perception)? If yes, how?

3. Has faculty use of the network changed teaching (Student perception)? If yes, how?

4. Has the network affected your workload or the distribution of time across teaching-related activities (e.g., office hours, tutoring) (Faculty perception)? If yes, how?

5. Has use of the network affected the quality of teaching material you use in the classroom (Faculty perception)? If yes, how?

6. Has the network affected your mentoring/advising relationships with students (Faculty perception)? If yes, how?

7. Has the network affected your confidence as a teacher (Faculty perception)? If yes, how?

8. Have you come to depend on the network for teaching (Faculty perception)? If yes, for what types of uses do you depend on the network for teaching?

9. Do you use the network for teaching preparation (Faculty perception)? If yes, how?

Network and Learning

1. Has the professor's use of the network affected your learning or understanding (Student perception)? If yes, how?

2. Has your use of the network affected the way you research and write papers (Student and librarian perception)? If yes, how?

    · Conceptualize topics
    · Gather cites
    · Obtain texts of articles
    · Write the paper

3. Has student use of the network affected the quality of their papers (Faculty and student perception)? If yes, how?

    · What is quality?
    · What specific aspects of quality have been affected?
    · How is this related to use of the network?

4. Has student use of the network affected grades (Faculty and student perception)? If yes, how?

5. Has the network affected your confidence as a student (Student perception)? If yes, how?

6. Have you come to depend on the network in your role as a student (Student perception)? If yes, for what do you depend on the network?

7. Has use of the network affected your delivery of (Faculty perception) or participation in (Student perception) distance learning courses or programs? If yes, in what ways?

8. Have specific network facilities or tools affected your learning (Student perception)? If yes, what are they?

9. Has the availability of specific network resources affected the curriculum (Faculty and student perception)? If yes, what are these resources?

Network and Research

1. Has the network affected the way you research and write a paper (Faculty, Ph. D. students' perception)? If yes, how? (This might include the gathering of citations, abstracts, and full texts of articles as well as the actual writing of the paper and communication with co-authors, editors, and reviewers.)

2. Has the network affected the way you conduct a research project (Faculty perception)? If yes, how?

    · Obtaining funding
    · Literature review (see above measure)
    · Carrying out research
    · Collaboration with colleagues
    · Publishing/publicizing results
    · Peer review
    · Dissertation review committee

Network and Recruitment

1. Does the network affect a potential faculty member's decision making process regarding an offer of employment (Faculty and administration perception)? If yes, how?

2. Does the network affect a potential student's decision making process regarding an offer of admission (Student and administration perception)? If yes, how?

3. Does the network affect institutional image and credibility (Faculty, student, and administration perception)? If yes, how?

Network and Administrative Tasks

1. Has the network changed the way you handle administrative tasks (Faculty and administrative staff perception)? If yes, how? Administrative tasks might include:

   • Creating class lists
   • Submitting grades
   • Planning conferences
   • Performing committee work
   • Performing tasks related to professional organizations

2. Has the network changed the way you handle administrative tasks (Student perception)? If yes, how? Administrative tasks might include:

   • Registering for classes
   • Obtaining housing
   • Obtaining meals
   • Dealing with the bursar's office
   • Obtaining financial aid
   • Finding a part-time job
   • Finding an internship or co-op
   • Finding a full-time job upon graduating
   • Finding information about graduate programs or other educational opportunities

3. Has the network affected the way you do your job (Administrative Staff perception)? If yes, how? Ways in which jobs may be affected might include:

   • Sharing files with other staff
   • Using online services for ordering supplies, making room reservations, arranging express deliveries
   • Communicating via email

4. Are there administrative tasks you would like to conduct via the network but which aren't currently possible (administrative staff perception)? If yes, what are they?

Network and Library Use

1. Has the network affected your use of electronic information resources (Faculty, student, and librarian perception)? If yes, how?

2. Has the network affected your ability to access information in the library (Faculty, student, and librarian perception)? If yes, how?

3. Has the library provided public access to the network (Faculty, student, and librarian perception)?

4. Has the network affected your ability to find the information you need in the library (Faculty, student, and librarian perception)? If yes, how?

5. Has the network affected the types of services provided by the library (Faculty, student and librarian perception)? If yes, how?

6. Has the library been involved in developing and providing access to campus information resources on the network (Faculty, student, and librarian perception)? If yes, how?

Network and Help Resources

1. Has the availability of help resources affected your use of the network (Faculty, student, and administrative staff)? If yes, which resources have affected your use and how? Help resources might include:

   • Workshops or classes on how to use a particular feature
   • Printed guides on how to use a particular feature
   • Online help available through email, newsgroups, or web sites
   • Walk-in help from a central help office
   • Telephone help from a central help office
   • Instructions from a distributed computer support person who works for your department or office
   • Help from friends

Network and the Campus Social/Cultural Environment

1. Has the network affected the social/cultural environment on campus (Faculty, student, and administrative staff perception)? If yes, how?

2. Do you receive information about clubs or recreational activities via the network (Faculty, student, and administrative staff perception)?

3. Do social or cultural organizations on campus use the network (Student, faculty, and administrative staff perception)?

4. Has the network changed the nature or frequency of your contact with others, both on and off the campus (Student, faculty, and administrative staff perception)? If yes, how?

Network and Professional Development

1. Has the network affected your professional development (Faculty and administrative staff perception)? If yes, how? The following activities might be considered professional development:

   • Participation in professional organizations
   • Self-directed learning, reading, and research
   • Development of new skills

2. How might the network be used for professional development (Faculty and administrative staff perception)?

Network and Collaboration

1. Has the network affected your involvement in collaborative activities (Faculty and staff perception)? If yes, how? Collaborative activities might include:

   • Projects with colleagues from other department or other institutions
   • Projects with commercial service providers and vendors
   • Projects with government agencies and other funding agencies
   • Participation with other institutions in consortia

2. How might the network be best designed to encourage collaboration both within the institution and with other institutions?

Strategies for Successful Evaluations

Successful data collection and evaluation, of any type, can be enhanced with some preliminary planning and thought. While the following list of suggestions is not intended to be comprehensive, evalu-

ators should keep these issues in mind as ways to increase the likelihood of a successful evaluation.

Knowing Your Audience

Prior to designing an evaluation and determining what data collection techniques will be used, it is important to recognize who the audience for the evaluation results will be. Potential audiences might be the users themselves, network managers, organizational administrators, boards of trustees, government policy makers, or others. A concern, however, is that different audiences may require different evaluation information. Thus, part of the evaluator's responsibility is to understand the information needs of the audience for whom the evaluation is being done. Some thought should be given to the measures, and thus the data collection techniques, that might be of special interest to that specific audience.

Deciding What Exactly will be Evaluated

Evaluators will not have the luxury of collecting and analyzing all the data they might want about a particular networked information service, due to lack of time, limited budget, inability to acquire the needed information, and a host of other reasons. Thus, they will have to define specific evaluation objectives. And, given the limitations, evaluators should focus on obtaining "actionable," results, i.e., affordable, feasible interventions or strategies which could be put in place to improve some aspect of the network.

Developing Additional Appropriate Indicators

Evaluators may also want to develop additional indicators specific to their networks, users, and institutions. For example, in the assessment of a part-time jobs database made available to the campus community from a particular server, it may be possible to establish the measure "number of students who found their jobs using the database." To use this performance measure, however, the evaluator will have to carefully define and operationalize key terms such as "found" and "jobs." Then, data collection techniques (selected from those listed above) would have to be considered in light of how well they would provide information on these two data elements.

Determining Costs and Schedules

For qualitative evaluations to be successful, they must be implemented in a timely fashion and with a clear sense of the funding required. In preparation for the evaluation, costs associated with standard budget items, e.g., personnel, supplies, travel, equipment, and contract services, should be identified. There is no use initiating an evaluation if there are inadequate resources available to complete it. It is better to complete a smaller, less costly evaluation than to attempt a large-scale evaluation and run out of funding during the process.

Equally important is developing a schedule for the completion of the project and detailing the key tasks that will have to be done over the duration of the study. There are many types of tasking charts and project management software programs currently available that can assist an evaluator with scheduling. Such scheduling insures that everyone involved in the project knows what tasks are to be completed by whom and when. Further, the scheduling allows the evaluator to monitor the progress of the evaluation more globally and effectively and identify possible problems while they can still be resolved.

Identifying the Appropriate Study Participants

One problem often encountered by new evaluators is in identifying appropriate participants. For example, in the evaluation of dial-up access to the network, simply collecting data from a random sample of network users may not produce enough participants who have actually used or know about the ability to dial into the campus network. The general rule of thumb is: do not expect users to provide you with information about things that they know nothing about!

Sometimes, obtaining the right mix of participants is critical. This concern is especially important in focus group sessions. If some members of the focus group are extremely knowledgeable about a particular network service and others are not, the group dialogue can be extremely skewed. One strategy is to carefully consider whether you need information from novice, intermediate, or expert network users. Another is to use a filter question in interviews and surveys to determine the type of user and his/her background before you proceed with collecting the information you require.

Developing, Pretesting, and Refining Data Collection Instruments

No data collection instrument should be administered without first being carefully developed, pretested, refined, and often pretested a second time. Qualitative data collection techniques require data collection instruments that make sense to the participants. One useful approach is to have the data collection instruments reviewed by (1) someone with experience in the data collection technique you wish to employ, and (2) a group of individuals who are members of the user group from which you will be obtaining the data.

Administering Instruments Appropriately

The logistics associated with administering data collection instruments can be formidable. Yet overlooking any of these details can seriously affect evaluation outcomes. Key concerns are: getting the full participation of all subjects, providing a forum for participants to discuss issues and concerns that the moderator does not bring up, and documenting participants' comments completely and accurately. To minimize these concerns, the following may be helpful:

- Arrange for a pleasant setting to conduct the focus group, surveys, transaction logs, interviews, etc., and typically, provide some refreshments and amenities

- Consider the order and development of topics to be discussed in the session

- Record and analyze the content of the session while it is occurring (e.g., use note takers, audio or video recorders, etc.)

- Manage and moderate the session in a positive and productive manner (prevent individuals from dominating or disrupting the session)

- Send follow-up thank you notes.

Once again, it is essential that these logistical concerns are considered and resolved within the data collection process.

Presenting Study Results and Findings

Evaluations incorporating qualitative data collection techniques typically fall under the heading of "action research," i.e., research that is intended to assist in the decision making process or assist in policy making. Thus, if the evaluation is to be successful, the findings have to be presented to decision makers in such a manner that (1) the decision makers are fully aware of the findings, (2) decision makers completely understand the findings, and (3) specific implications and recommendations are made explicit.

Summary

Users of this manual can make the most effective use of this section by combining these qualitative data collection techniques with other data collection techniques presented later in the manual. None of these techniques alone will tell the entire story, but the combination of these techniques can provide a valid, reliable, and rich picture of academic networking.

Manual users should expect to customize their data collection efforts to their own networks, users, and institutions. Some of the techniques described here may be more useful in some situations than in others. Likewise, some of the topics and issues suggested for investigation may be more appropriate in some situations than in others. Evaluators should consider the techniques and topics described here to be a menu from which they can select items most appropriate to their environments and interests.

PART III:

MEASURES

This section of the manual describes a number of measures to assess the academic networked environment. They are organized under the broader categories of users, costs, network traffic, use, services, and support.

Each measure includes a definition, a discussion of issues that the institution may need to address when collecting data for that measure, some general procedures to consider in collecting and analyzing the data, and some suggestions for additional measures. Example data collection forms for some of the measures are provided in Appendix B. Like the techniques discussed in the previous section, these measures should be considered as a menu from which evaluators can pick those that are most useful at their particular institution.

USERS

Network Users

- Count of Network Users

- Count of Active Network Users

Definition

Basic measures critical to describing the use of and activity on the network include a Count of Network Users (CNU) and Count of Active Network Users (CANU). The CNU is defined as the number of email accounts with access to the campus network. The CANU is defined as the number of email accounts that have logged onto the network during a specified period of time. The use of both measures distinguishes between those who are authorized to use the system and those who are authorized *and* actually use the network. A tally and analysis of email accounts as a basis for identifying the number of users and active users is suggested because it is a widely-used network application at many higher education institutions.

Issues

Before CNU and CANU can be determined, network administrators and others in the academic institution must discuss a number of key issues and reach agreement on policies to produce these counts. These issues include the following:

- Defining "the network." For purposes of these counts we recommend that the campus network be defined as those telecommunications services and resources over which the academic institution has primary responsibility and control. In some instances, however, the campus may have multiple "backbone" networks.

- Defining users. More accurate methods to identify network users other than email accounts may exist, depending on the record-keeping techniques used at a particular institution, e.g., user IDs, official registrations, or payroll records. If so, users of the manual may wish to employ these methods.

- Including distributed computing accounts. Many academic networks include distributed, multiple servers that have their own administration and email accounts. Thus, a decision must be made whether to include only centrally administered email accounts or to include email accounts from distributed servers when calculating the CNU and CANU.

- Purging inactive accounts. The accuracy of the CNU will depend on the institution's policy regarding purging inactive accounts. Policies should be in place that regularly purge accounts from the files for those who are no longer authorized to use the network.

- Defining authorized users in the campus networking community. There may be significant numbers of individuals with email accounts on the campus system who are "guests" and do not belong to the campus community but use the network, e.g., students who graduate but continue using the network for mail and other applications. Decisions must be made to consistently count the "bona fide" members of the campus networking community.

Further, it may be unclear how to determine who is "faculty" or "students" or "staff" or "other" types of users. Definitions for such user types may need to be agreed upon before the CNU and CANU can be analyzed by user type.

- Defining what constitutes an "active user." For purposes of CANU we recommend that an active user is one who has shown any network activity on his/her email account in a preceding one-month period. This definition recog-

nizes that it is possible for some users to access a network service without using an email account and thus, the longer time period may alleviate an underestimation of some network use. Institutions may wish to define a different time period for defining "active user."

- Maintaining privacy. As a general principle, safeguards should be created to ensure that individual names are not identified, or that particular uses of the network are not linked with individuals.

- Identifying multiple email accounts. Some individuals on campuses with multiple servers may have multiple email accounts. Thus, the number of email accounts is not the same as the number of individuals with email accounts. The results from an analysis of "email accounts" will differ from an analysis of "individuals with email accounts." For a better resolution of the CNU and CANU some institutions might wish to sample users to determine the average percentage who have multiple accounts.

Data Collection

Once the above issues are addressed and resolved in a formal policy, the institution can calculate the CNU and CANU. The system administrators, who maintain a registration list of all those email accounts that have been allocated to date, can provide a count of those individuals on that registration list. The CNU can include central system email accounts and accounts registered on distributed servers.

In order to determine the CANU, network administrators will need to develop a software program for the various servers that maintains a record of the first instance a particular email account shows activity during a sample one-month period (see Appendix C). At the end of the sample one-month period, the network administrator counts the number of instances when different email accounts were recorded as "active." This sample one-month period should be a "typical" time period during the academic year.

Depending on the situation, other data collection techniques may be possible. For example, some institutions may maintain transaction logs of all campus email logins during a given time period. If such a log exists, an analysis of those logins that removes duplicate logins would also produce a count of active users during that predetermined one-month period.

Data Analysis

The analysis of the data for both the CNU and CANU provides a count of the number and type of email logins. The CNU and CANU can be analyzed in greater detail depending on the records maintained by users of the manual or others on campus. For example, both measures might be broken down by:

- Undergraduate users
- Graduate users
- Faculty users
- Staff users
- Other users

Different institutions may require different data collection techniques to produce these counts. The most straight forward approach is to compare the list of email accounts collected from the CNU and CANU to a registration list or to another official list that includes "status" of the holders of the email accounts. Users of the manual would then write a program to analyze the status of email account holders and categorize those accounts by the above categories or other categories available in the registration files.

Discussion

The CNU and CANU are basic and key descriptors of the number of email accounts currently on the network and the number of accounts in active use. These counts are a method for users of the manual to track, on a longitudinal basis, the growth (or decline) in network users. It is important to recognize that these counts do not describe the type of use being made of the network. Other measures, such as counts of telnet sessions, FTP sessions, access to WWW sites, etc. would be necessary. Additional software may be necessary to maintain these other counts.

Although there are numerous issues, as described above, that must be resolved before calculating and analyzing CNU and CANU, these are important and very useful measures. Other analyses, such as cost

per user or cost per use of the network cannot be computed without first computing CNU and CANU.

Additional Suggestions

Some institutions may be able to compute (1) the Percentage of Official Service Community with email accounts, (2) Percentage of Official Service Community that does not have an email account, (3) Percentage of Official Service Community that has an email account but did not log-in during the sample time period, and (4) Percentage of Official Service Community with Active Email Accounts. The measure compares the total available number of legal institutional members to those using the network. Such a measure assumes that:

- The number of active email users reflects the number of active *network* users.

- The institution can produce a count of the official members in the academic community, typically defined as students, staff, faculty, and other.

- Network administrators can equate the CNU and CANU from email accounts to individuals. This would require some corrections of the CNU and CANU for holders of multiple email accounts.

This measure is a starting point for campuses to use as an indicator of the percentage of individuals associated with the campus that (1) have email accounts, and (2) are active users of those email accounts.

COSTS

Technology Expenditures

- Annual Information Technology Expenditures

Definition

Annual Information Technology Expenditures (AITE) is defined as the total amount of money spent by the academic institution on information technology (IT) for the most recent fiscal year.

Issues

The method used to compute this measure may vary among institutions. Calculating this measure will require discussion among network administrators and other institutional officials that leads to agreement on a number of issues.

- <u>Defining IT Cost Categories and Elements within those Categories</u>. Academic institutions may include different cost categories as part of total IT expenditures. Typical IT cost categories include:

  - System/server hardware
  - Communications hardware
  - Vendor installation and licensing fees
  - Software
  - Training and education
  - Wiring
  - Facilities upgrades and maintenance
  - Content and resource development for network services
  - Program planning and management
  - Staffing
  - Internet service provider

This list is illustrative only. Specific types of expenditures within these, or additional basic categories, must be defined and described by each institution. Institutions may wish to refer to existing institutional budget categories, or cost categories identified in the annual CAUSE and NACUBO surveys (see Appendix C).

- <u>Including Departmental and Other Units in the AITE</u>. IT expenditures can originate from many organizational units on campus. These include the centrally administered computing services intended for the entire organization, as well as individual departments and other units on campus. The AITE can be based on:

  - Central computing services expenditures only
  - Central computing services expenditures AND departmental/other units expenditures.

The choice of what to base the AITE on is likely to depend on the nature of the budgeting system in place at a particular institution and the degree to which such expenditures can be tracked and monitored at the departmental level.

- <u>Identifying IT Expenditures</u>. Before calculating IT expenditures, a method must be developed that identifies the various IT expenditures. Some IT expenditures may be bundled as part of other expenditures, some units may wish to exclude such expenses for political reasons, or some expenditures may not be included in appropriate IT budget lines or accounts. Institutional procedures and policies may need to be created to increase the likelihood that all IT expenditures are identified. Academic organizations must identify and define these cost elements consistently across campus and over time for the measure to be reliable.

- <u>Recognizing Shared Costs or Contributions From a Consortia</u>. A complicated issue in computing IT expenditures is identifying and quantifying expenditures that support consortia memberships that may provide certain types of services, resources, or equipment. The institution may either wish to state as policy that such expenditures will not be included as part of overall IT expenditures or, state specifically what will and will not be included.

- <u>Capital Expenditures and Operating Expenses</u>. Capital expenditures for hardware and software, with a useful life of more than one fiscal year, may be annualized over their life cycle. Accounting procedures may already be in place to deal with this issue or procedures may need to be developed.

Data Collection

Methods for calculating the AITE are likely to vary from campus to campus, but one basic approach to computing it is first to resolve the issues identified above. Resolution may require a number of meetings with key institutional officials knowledgeable about the issues.

Based on those decisions, a network administrator or other institutional official (the Chief Financial Officer) would conduct an analysis of the institution's budget to identify specific account numbers or budget lines within which such expenditures are expected to occur. Once these accounts are identified, the official would obtain the total expenditures for each account and total them to obtain the AITE.

Some institutions may already have a database or MIS in place that identifies and tracks certain types of expenditures. In such instances the design of the database should be reviewed to insure that all accounts with IT expenditures have been identified and are included in the database. Other institutions may find it useful and appropriate to develop such a database to monitor and analyze institutional IT expenditures.

Data Analysis

The analysis procedure produces a count of total IT expenditures from various budgetary resources available on campus. The budget information can be grouped in terms of specific categories of expenditures (as listed above). These expenditures, both as an overall total and within specific categories, can be tracked over time to determine trends. Expenditures can also be analyzed in terms of the departments or units receiving and spending the monies.

Discussion

The accuracy of the AITE will depend on the conscientiousness with which the institution defines IT expenditures, its ability to monitor and track those expenditures in a database, and success in securing the involvement of all departmental units in identifying and tracking the expenditures within IT accounts. It is likely, however, that a number of IT expenditures will not be identified and cannot be tracked. For example, some individuals or units may either hide or fail to recognize IT expenditures. Such inaccuracies in the AITE are likely to occur. Nonetheless, an estimate of AITE which is computed from consistently defined cost categories and based on "best information" is better than no estimate.

Tracking the AITE is important in providing longitudinal information on the growth or decline of IT expenditures at a particular institution. This measure, however, becomes more interesting in light of other information such as (1) the degree to which both institutional and departmental IT, networking, or telecommunications goals and objectives are being accomplished, and (2) the degree to which users of the network are satisfied with the reliability of the infrastructure and the quality of the services and applications provided (see user survey in Part IV).

The longitudinal expenditure trends may be considered in the context of overall declining costs for certain information technologies and services. Nonetheless, the trends that such measures identify may be more valuable than one-time snapshots of expenditures.

Additional Suggestions

Once the database of institutional IT expenditures is developed, a number of additional types of analyses can be completed. The AITE is especially useful for calculating IT expenditures as a percentage of all institutional expenditures:

$$\frac{Annual\ Information\ Technology\ Expenditures}{Annual\ Institutional\ Expenditures}$$

Network administrators may wish to track the changes in the AITE over time; the AITE as a percentage of all institutional expenditures over time; or the relative percentage of specific types of IT expenditures that are allocated to hardware as opposed to training and education, etc.

Another important application of the AITE is to produce measures that relate total IT expenditures to the number of official individuals whom the institution serves. Examples of such measures are IT expenditures per capita which can be computed by:

$$\frac{Annual\ Information\ Technology\ Expenditures}{Total\ Official\ Institutional\ Population\ Served}$$

Or, annual expenditures per active user, calculated by:

$$\frac{Annual\ Information\ Technology\ Expenditures}{CANU}$$

To calculate these measures, the institution must have a count of its official population served — typically in terms of students, faculty, staff, and others. The measure would estimate the amount of IT expenditures being spent per person. The measure could also analyze expenditures by type of individuals, i.e., students, faculty, staff, and other groups of users.

Some institutions with experience in IT cost data collection and analysis compute and track more than thirty ratios of various kinds. These include IT costs per student or per faculty; costs per connections on campus; IT-related salaries as a percentage of all institutional salaries, etc. The initial undertaking for the institution must be the definition of cost categories and primary data collection. Actual measures used at an institution will depend on resource availability, experience, and desire to link IT expenditures to other institutional activities, goals, and services.

NETWORK TRAFFIC

Network Traffic Measures

- Router Traffic as a Measure of Overall Campus Network Activity

- Modem Traffic into the Campus Network

- Internet Traffic

General Comments

Key elements in assessing overall network performance are measures of the physical configuration of the campus network and the traffic it carries. These measures can be used to provide support in planning for network expansion and the associated budget process. They also provide feedback on network quality through analysis of blockages and delays.

Measurements in this category are generally analyzed by reviewing trends in traffic flow. Disruptions to the normality of these trends indicate changes in user behavior or difficulties in network performance. It is challenging to predict how new applications might affect bandwidth requirements, but ongoing measurement schemes should provide early warnings and adjustment opportunities prior to service deterioration.

A secondary benefit of these traffic measurements is a better understanding of the day-to-day network operations and maintenance functions. Individual network failures can be pinpointed and corrected more efficiently when overall network surveillance and measurements are part of the normal methods of operation. Expenditures associated with traffic measurements deserve high priority because of their benefit in planning and decision making.

The amount of centralization in network service provision and control will have a profound effect on the ability to measure and assess traffic flow within the institution. In a highly centralized environment, data collection and analysis are facilitated by a campus-wide, well planned and coordinated network, administered from a central location. A decentralized environment with individual networks, often of different technical and operational designs, makes traffic flow analysis difficult. Nonetheless, in either situation some fundamental traffic measurements will provide a basis for trend analysis and quality assessment of the network.

Issues

- Knowledge of the Existing Network. Before network traffic measures can be computed, users of the manual must first be able to describe the existing network environment, be aware of the various components configuring the network, and understand linkages between and among the network components.

- Cooperative Data Collection. To calculate traffic measures in a distributed environment cooperation and coordination of measurement efforts among the various network officials will be essential.

- Unique services offered by the institution. A Web site, for example, that attracts international access can have significant impacts on traffic measures. Institutional officials may wish to better familiarize themselves with such unique services provided to external net users.

- Peak versus Least Usage. Many institutions will be especially interested in traffic measures that identify "peak usage" and "least usage" times during the day or for special times during the year. The institution will need to define peak and least usage for their particular situation.

These issues may need to be discussed and resolved prior to calculating the measures discussed below.

Router Traffic as a Measure of Overall Campus Network Activity

Definition

In the campus environment, local area networks (LANs) are connected to each other and to off-campus networks through routers. By measuring and analyzing the traffic moving through these routers, it is possible to obtain meaningful usage information about the overall campus network. The usefulness of this measure is its ability to analyze usage trends over time. The unit of measurement can be data packets or bytes, carried on the network over a defined time interval. In some cases these routers are centralized in a common location with direct fiber or coaxial connections to the various sub-networks scattered about the university environment. From this router "pool," connections are made to computers acting as servers and to the Internet.

In other cases the routers may not be centralized but interconnected in some manner that consolidates access to common servers and to the Internet. Data collection, which takes place at each router location, is the same in either case but is greatly facilitated in the centralized router configuration.

Data Collection

1. Identify the campus network architecture with emphasis on the location of routers and their connectivity to common servers and to the Internet. Detailed network mapping will be valuable for this measure and should be done with as much accuracy as possible. Many network departments already have access to such detailed maps.

2. Investigate router interconnectivity and develop a strategy to measure router traffic. Most routers have built-in data gathering capabilities. Where this is not the case, the use of external network analyzers is recommended (see Appendix D for additional information). The size of packets is determined by the specific network application and/or the associated data link protocol and will vary over the campus environment. Thus, the traffic measurement should include packet quantities as well as some assessment of packet size or protocol. As an alternative, byte counts may be used.

3. Ideally, traffic measurements would be gathered constantly and consistently. If this is not feasible, select a sample period of one to two weeks for measuring network traffic. Select a "typical" period — preferably two weeks. Do not select a time period that might result in an exceptionally heavy or light traffic load. During this interval, packet or byte counts should be recorded every five minutes. This measurement should be repeated each semester and the data should be recorded for trend analysis.

4. Investigate the measurement capability of each router and install any necessary software to accomplish data collection (see Appendix D). For those router locations without internal data diagnostics, provide external network analyzers. If this data collection method is technically or financially difficult, a less precise but also informative approach to investigate traffic flows and possible delays is to use questions in the user survey, described in Part IV.

Data Analysis

For the selected time period, the quantity of measured data packets, or bytes, will be used as a measure of overall network activity. Total counts on a daily or weekly basis will provide a measure of usage growth, while the five-minute counts will provide indications of busy periods. These statistics can then be used in conjunction with user satisfaction data (see user survey) and cost statistics.

The best presentation method for this data is a visual plot. Annual plots of daily traffic volumes will show trends and effects of network additions and reconfiguration. Daily plots of five-minute interval data will indicate peak load periods and network congestion. Semester-long and year-long plots are also useful in analyzing network traffic and identifying trends.

Discussion

Although tracking measurements of router traffic over time will provide an assessment of network growth, it must be recognized that changes in network configuration will affect packet counts. As a network grows, additional routers are provided to keep each sub-network at a reasonable size. As more routers are added, inter-router traffic, by design, creates more packets. In analyzing trends, network reconfiguration must be incorporated into the analysis.

Differences in network architecture at various locations make generalization of traffic statistics difficult. Further study and experimentation in this area may be needed before specific analysis techniques can be recommended. Traffic versus capacity measures, however, are especially important in planning network developments.

The counting of packets is network specific but not application specific. Traffic trends can be measured and analyzed in any given network over time, but within that network there is no simple way to determine which application created which specific packets.

Modem Traffic into the Campus Network

- Dial-up User Rate

- Saturation Rate

Definition

Dial-up user rate is the number of users that dial-up to the campus network from remote locations during a given time period. Saturation rate is the percentage of time that all modem ports are in use and is one indicator of the extensiveness of remote network use.

Most campus networks allow faculty, students, and staff to connect to the network remotely by using modems. There are a number of measures related to modem traffic into the campus network that can be calculated. A measure of this traffic provides an indication of the amount of use off-campus, or from on-campus locations without direct network connectivity.

Data Collection

Approach 1: (for Dial-up User Rate)

1. Identify the total number of modem ports available for remote connection to the campus computing network. Each group of ports should have a designated telephone number.

2. Select an appropriate sampling period. Ideally, data would be collected constantly and consistently. Typically this would be done by recording port activity every five minutes. Where this is not feasible, the sampling period should represent a "typical" period of at least one week and preferably two weeks, and should be repeated each semester. Do not select a time period that might result in an exceptionally heavy or light number of dial-up requests from users.

3. Install software that can monitor individual port activity and can record, for each five-minute period during the 24 hour day, the busy or idle condition of each port (see Appendix D). It may be important to differentiate between SLIP/PPP access versus terminal emulation. An individual record will be created for each port as well as a record of total activity in each group of ports, and of the total dial-in network.

4. Install software that counts the number of dial-ins for all modem ports during the specified sample period.

Approach 2: (for Saturation Rate)

Develop software that regularly dials-in to the campus on selected phone lines, at sample time periods and records the number of times it makes a connection versus the times it is unable to make a connection. The software maintains a record of the time of day when called and whether the result was a connection or a non-connection.

Data Analysis

1. For each port, determine the percentage of time during each twenty-four hour period that the port was in use. There are 288 five-minute periods during a day. For each of those five minute periods, the software calculates the actual time that the port was busy. These calculations are then averaged over the one day time period. Some institutions may wish to sample only selected five minute periods throughout the day — say every other five-minute period producing 144 sample time periods rather than 288. The results from this measure will range from 0 to 100%.

2. Determine any times during the entire study period when all ports in a specific group were simultaneously busy. This is most easily done by plotting the total port occupancy, for all five-minute samples, over the study period and examining the peaks in relation to the maximum port occupancy. Determine the percentage of time during each twenty-four hour period that an "all ports busy" condition occurred and the specific times of such conditions.

3. An analysis of data related to user dial-up rate can be accomplished by simply counting the number of dial-ups for specific periods of time — by hour, a group of hours, by day, or by month. Officials may wish to compare dial-up user rates for specific periods of time, say evenings or weekends, or they may only wish to produce average use over a monthly period. Once again, plotting the number of dial-up users over time is likely to be most useful for trend analysis.

Discussion

The most important measure is the "all ports busy" condition. This can seriously affect the users' ability to access the network and their perception of quality of service. These results can be compared with data from the user survey which, in part, assess users' perceptions. A number of factors may affect or cause the "all ports busy" condition:

• The system may need additional computer ports, modems, or incoming telephone lines.

• Individual modems or computer ports may not be performing properly. The router traffic measure described above will help to point out those problems by showing an abnormal pattern of use on individual ports. Furthermore, some ports may exhibit a constant busy condition indicating an inability to release. Also, some ports may show abnormally low activity indicating a problem in port access from the public telephone network.

• Problems in direct access to the network from on-campus locations may cause users to revert to dial-in access. Abnormal increases in dial-up use may indicate such a condition. Times when all modem ports are busy and the on-campus network is experiencing difficulty do not necessarily indicate a need for additional dial-in arrangements.

• Extension or expansion of the on-campus direct access network may cause a reduction in dial-in traffic. As additional residence halls are directly connected and existing on-campus public access locations are expanded, the need for dial-in access may decrease. Use of the modem pool should be considered against direct access on the overall traffic load.

Additional Suggestions

Since dial-up access is obtained through the telephone network, either via an on-campus PBX or through the local telephone company central office, it is not readily determined from where the call originated. Some investigative work in this area, however, could indicate on-campus locations in need of new or additional direct connections. For example, these data could be used to prioritize wiring of student housing locations. Data gathering of this type would require use of special software and the Automatic Number Identification feature of the telephone network. Another approach might be to include a prompt at initial connection which queries users as to their status/location.

As modem speeds increase and prices continue to drop, the campus-based modem pool may be upgraded and users of the dial-in access service can be encouraged to purchase modems of the highest affordable speeds. These higher speed modems may reduce an individual's time needed for dial-up access per session, thus providing more access to the network.

Internet Traffic

• Incoming Internet Volume

• Outgoing Internet Volume

• Saturation

Definition

Internet traffic is a measure of incoming and outgoing data, between the campus network and the Internet access provider, over a given sample period. The traffic activity can be measured by packets or bytes. This information can be used to assess the adequacy of the connecting facility and to track Internet traffic as a function of time.

Saturation is a measure of the extent to which campus Internet circuit capacity is being used for a given period of time.

Data Collection

1. Identify the number and traffic handling capacity of transmission facilities (e.g., circuits) that connect the university-based network to the Internet. These are usually, but not restricted to, 56 kilobit per second, 1.544 megabit per second, and 45 megabit per second facilities. Various terms are interchangeable when referring to these circuits. 56 kilobit circuits may be called Switchway or Digital Data Service (DDS), 1.544 megabit circuits may be called T1's or DS-1's, while 45 megabit circuits are commonly referred to as DS-3's. Higher speed circuits, in the SONET family, at 51.840 megabits per second, and multiples thereof, are likely to become common in the near future.

2. Select an appropriate sampling period. Ideally, data collection should take place constantly and consistently on each of the Internet connections. Where this is not feasible, the sampling period should represent a "typical" time of at least one week and preferably two weeks, and should be repeated each semester. Do not select a time period that might result in an exceptionally heavy or light amount of Internet traffic.

3. Install software to monitor activity on the circuit(s) and to record the actual number of packets or bytes entering and leaving the campus. This software should also be able to calculate the saturation rate, i.e., the circuit occupancy as a percentage of total circuit capacity. It is recommended that sample data be taken at five-minute intervals throughout the study period.

Data Analysis

1. Determine the saturation rate by comparing the packets or bytes entering or leaving the network to the capacity of the circuit for packets or bytes in a given time period for each of the samples and plot this data for the entire study period. Results from this measure will range from 0 and 100% for each sample which occurs at five-minute intervals.

2. Determine any times during the study period when the connecting facility is at or near full capacity. A threshold of 95% can be used to indicate possible overflow conditions.

Discussion

The most important indicator resulting from this data collection is the "circuit at full capacity" condition. This can seriously affect the user's ability to connect to the Internet, or can slow down the data exchange to an unacceptable level. There are a number of factors that can cause such a condition:

• The Internet connection may simply have too little bandwidth to accommodate the needs of the campus.

• The Internet connection may not be performing properly. In the case of digital circuitry, a check of bi-polar violations or framing slips can indicate potential or real problems resulting in reduced throughput. Since these Internet circuits are provided by telecommunications vendors, coordination with them is essential to insure proper performance. Although most Internet providers follow preventative maintenance procedures and line monitoring, it is suggested that campus-based surveillance also be developed.

USE

Frequency of Email Use

• Percentage of Frequent Email Users

• Percentage of Infrequent Email Users

Definition

Frequent network users are those individuals who send and/or receive a pre-determined number of messages in a sample three-day period. Infrequent network users are those individuals who send and/or receive a predetermined number of messages or fewer during the sample period. Institutions may wish to use different criteria for "frequent" versus "infrequent." A beginning break point might be 50 messages or more for frequent users and fewer than 50 for infrequent users. The measures are described by the following computation:

$$\frac{\textit{Number of Frequent Network Users}}{\textit{Count of Network Users}}$$

$$\frac{\textit{Number of Infrequent Network Users}}{\textit{Count of Network Users}}$$

Issues

- Network Use versus Email Use. In some academic settings use of the network may be accomplished without an email account. In such instances, the count of network user (CNU) used to compute this measure will underestimate actual use.

- Criteria for Frequent versus Infrequent Use. Depending on the average number of messages sent and received per person at individual institutions, the definition of "frequent" and "infrequent" may be better decided by a number other than 50.

Data Collection

Many universities have a central server which allows for the creation of new email and collection/storing of incoming email. If an institution has email traffic which utilizes distributed servers, the institution must determine how it wants to collect data for each server as well as the central computing system. The procedures for gathering data from a distributed server will be the same as for the central server.

Select an appropriate sampling period to monitor the email traffic. The sampling period should represent a "typical" time during a two-week period. During that two- week period sample at least three, three-day periods. Do not select a time period that might result in exceptionally heavy or light use. The institution may wish to monitor email traffic two or three times a year to have an accurate count of use as well as to see user trends.

Approach 1: (Activity Log)

Conduct a random sample of the user population from each category of faculty, staff, graduate, undergraduate, and ask participants to keep an accurate activity log of the number of times they send and/or receive email during the data collection period (see Appendix B.1 for a sample log).

In designing this activity log, additional information may be included such as the length of time that email was accessed, the number of messages sent and received, and the types of messages: personal, professional, etc. Users of the log should receive some training or instruction on how to complete the log.

Approach 2: (Software Management System)

Install a software management system on the central server (and, if desired, on each distributed server) that can monitor e-mail traffic (see Appendix D). (Some mail servers automatically maintain transaction logs.) Set this system to count the number of times that each user (or a sample of users) sent AND/OR received an email message during the data collection period.

Data Analysis

Both the activity log and the software management system result in data sets indicating the number of times that an email message was sent and/or received during the sample period. The analyst computes the number of instances that a particular individual sent and/or received an email message.

If an activity log is used, users can be subdivided by status: faculty, staff, graduate, undergraduate, and other groups. The number of frequent and infrequent users for each category can also be calculated. Some software management systems may also allow for type of analysis if the network administrator has included user status as part of their email file space name.

Using the campus email directory (if one exists) may be the best way to identify a sample of individuals to either maintain the activity log or to monitor subjects automatically. An effort should be made, however, to insure that the directory is current and that users are not systematically excluded (due to their own choosing, lack of directory updating, or other reasons). The directory also can be useful for subdividing the user population by type.

Discussion

Data collected for calculating frequency of email use should be monitored closely to insure that there is a reasonable distribution in the number of individuals who "qualify" for inclusion in each group. If, for example, 75% of all those sampled qualify as frequent users, evaluators may wish to redefine the criteria for being considered a frequent user on that particular campus.

Additional Suggestions

Knowing the number of frequent and infrequent users will be important in assessing the impact of the network on the academic institution. Additional analysis correlating, for example, grade point average (GPA) with frequent student users, and funding for frequent faculty users could be developed using this baseline number of frequent users.

Another measure that may be of interest to some institutions is the ratio between the number of email messages sent by users of the network versus the number received during a specific time period. Such a measure provides an indication of the degree to which email from non-campus users affects overall traffic. For example, during a 24 hour period, if 5,000 email messages are sent by campus users and 9,000 are received, there is a net traffic income from outside the campus.

It may be possible to link the frequent and infrequent users to responses to the user survey (see Section IV). For example, if the activity logs identify a pool of frequent users, those same users could then be surveyed to obtain information regarding their overall satisfaction levels on various network services. The same might be done with infrequent users. Comparing frequent versus infrequent users' levels of satisfaction may provide useful clues for improving selected networked services.

Use of Clusters or Public Sites to Access the Network

- Ratio of Network Users to Available Public Terminals

- Occupancy Rate of Public Sites

Definition

Public clusters will be defined as those locations that the institution has created for public use of the academic network by individuals who are authorized through the use of log-in identification and passwords. The users may be students, faculty, or staff of the institution.

These clusters provide access to network-based applications such as, but not limited to, email, the Internet, wordprocessing, databases, spreadsheets, and statistical analysis tools. This measurement will address the extent to which the institution provides such access, on a per user basis, trends in that user per terminal statistic, and the actual use of the public cluster terminals.

Data Collection

1. Obtain the Count of Network Users (CNU) and Count of Active Network Users (CANU) as described earlier.

2. Obtain a count of the public cluster sites and number of terminals or workstations at each site. At most institutions this will be most readily obtained from the centralized academic computing personnel. In other institutions, the public clusters may be provided at individual departments, in student housing, or in other locations.

3. For each cluster obtain the schedule of hours of operation during a typical academic week.

4. In most instances, each cluster has an assistant or supervisor on duty during the hours of operation. This person can be assigned responsibility for maintaining a manual log of workstation occupancy during a sampling period. Select a sampling period of one week, and preferably two weeks, during which the cluster attendant will record workstation occupancy at 30-minute intervals. This sample period should be the same for all clusters within the environment of the institution.

5. If no monitor is available, an alternative occupancy record may be created through a user sign-in/sign-out log (see Appendix B.2). Upon entering the cluster facility a user signs in and enters the time of entry. The time of exit from the facility is also recorded.

Data Analysis

The primary measures will be ratios of Network Users (both CNU and CANU) to available public terminals. These measures can be compared to established benchmarks, based on ratios at similar institutions, or they can be accumulated over time to track the changes in the ratio.

For each cluster the percent occupancy may be computed for each 30 minute check point during the sample period. These occupancy statistics can be summarized graphically for each cluster and for the total of all clusters.

Discussion

If the institution provides network access in dormitory rooms, the need for public access will be reduced. The establishment and expansion of public clusters should be directly linked to plans for individual network access.

Occupancy statistics count users seated at workstation locations or users who have signed into the cluster environment. There is an assumed high correlation between these counts and actual network use.

Network Applications

- Count of "Hits" on Applications

- Use of Applications by Specific User Groups

Definition

These measures produce a count of how often specific applications are used during a given sample period. The measures can also produce data regarding the type of person who uses the application and for what period of time.

Introduction

Institutions can make applications available to their users from a server which is networked to individual desktop computers via a local area network (LAN). Servers usually require special software or code in order to count "hits" on an application. The type of special software a server needs for counting application use depends on the network operating system which controls the server.

Some users may receive their applications from more than one server or mainframe. For instance, a department administrator may receive her word processing applications from her department's LAN server drive, her e-mail from a central university Unix mail server, access to payroll entry screens from a mainframe, and desktop publishing applications from her desktop computer's hard drive. Given this complicated scenario, it may be difficult to obtain an accurate count of campus-wide use of a given application. However, come counts can be obtained by making use of one of the following two methods: application metering software or user activity logs.

Data Collection: Counting Hits

Software can be used on some servers and mainframes to determine how often an application is used (see Appendix D). The ability of a server or mainframe to run software which can count hits on an application depends on many network configuration factors that this manual does not address. Each institution will have to consult with its networking staff to determine how it can best support counting software.

1. Select the applications for which you wish to obtain usage data.

2. Determine which servers/mainframes provide access to those applications.

3. Determine which operating system resides on those servers.

4. Determine which application counting software program will work with which operating system.

5. Install the above software.

6. Choose a test period which represents a period of "typical" network usage. Do not choose a period when demand for an application will be unusually heavy or light.

7. Run the software and obtain report of data.

Issues

- Inability to Measure All Applications. This method cannot measure what applications users are using from their hard drives and may not be able to measure use of *all* applications available over the network.

- Use of the Application. Application counting software cannot distinguish who uses the application, or how many different people use the application, but can say how many times the application was used. For the most part, software tracking will not reveal what category of user uses the application (i.e. faculty, staff, student).

- System Performance. Running software metering applications may reduce the performance of the server.

- Distributed Access to Applications. Because of the distributed architecture of many campus LANs, the same application resides on many different servers across campus. Placing the software on all servers which offer the application in question may require the cooperation of distributed computing units which control those servers not under the management of the central computing services unit.

Discussion

As an alternative, use of the manual can select servers for analysis. One method might be to only measure the demand for applications on servers which service public computer clusters. Another method would be to randomly select a given number of campus servers or select several servers from the major categories of server, and then measure application demand on them. For instance, select one server which serves the public computing clusters, one server that serves administrative offices, and one server that belongs to a distributed unit.

Data Collection: Activity Log

Alternatively, users of this manual can conduct a random or quota sampling of the user population to recruit a non-biased pool of participants. Researchers would ask the participants to keep a log of what applications they used during the sampling period, the length of time they used it, and if appro-

priate, the purpose of use (e.g., research, teaching, class activities, personal, or entertainment). Sample participants should receive some training in how to complete the log. Appendix B.3 provides an example of such a log.

Issues

- User Response. Activity logs are successful data collection tools only if the log users are fully committed to the project. Users of the manual must select a sample group of committed users who represent the spectrum of people at that particular campus.

- Training. The quality of the data recorded on the log is likely to improve if participants receive training in how to complete the log and are given the opportunity to ask questions about the process.

- Transparency of Networked Applications. Given the transparency of some networked applications and services, individuals may not be able to determine when, or if, they have begun or ended a particular application.

Analysis

Once the data have been collected they can be analyzed to calculate the number of times a particular network application has been "hit" by a user within a given time period. It is important, however, to recognize that the number of hits may mean only that the application was viewed and never actually used.

It may also be important to determine the times of day when certain applications are in greater or lesser demand. Such demand periods may affect the response time in using the application or may suggest peak demand times when it may not be possible to access the application. This information could be especially useful if the application is licensed to accommodate only a given number of users at a certain time.

Discussion

Both the software management system and the activity log result in data indicating the number of times users accessed an application across a network. The software management system provides more accurate quantitative information regarding the total number of hits on an application during the sampling period, but for the most part cannot provide information regarding the users, the length of time they used the application, or what they used it for. Using the log approach, the analyst can subdivide the number of hits on an application by user category, by the length of time used, and by reason for using.

These data, combined with qualitative data regarding users' opinions and perceptions of the importance of applications, can provide insightful information regarding the impact of the network applications. The analyst could further combine this data with data regarding GPA or grants received to suggest which applications seem to improve student performance.

Additional Suggestions

Users of the manual may wish to experiment with "pop up" electronic questionnaires that appear on the users' screen after they hit a particular application. The questionnaire could have a number of short easy questions about the user's reasons for requesting this application, their assessment of the application, and why they are using this particular application.

Counts of the types of network applications and services hit by users will vary from campus to campus. In some situations, users of the manual may be especially interested in counts of Internet-related applications such as telnet, Web, or FTP sessions. In other institutions, counts of the use of locally mounted applications, data bases, or other services may be of interest.

Users of this manual can benefit by combining data from these two measures with qualitative data that show which applications users consider most important to their academic needs. The combination of quantitative and qualitative data provides insight into how the campus network is used, and also to help in planning what applications to offer in the future.

Internet Access to Shared Servers

- Count of Accesses via Commercial Provider

- Count of Accesses via Dial-up Connection

Definition

These counts provide an indication of the extent to which users access campus servers via the Internet and the extent to which that access results from direct dial-up access or via a commercial provider.

Background

Many universities offer the campus community access to e-mail and other programs on shared servers, servers which many departments or sub-units share. Given the growing demand for off-campus, or remote access to these servers and services, institutions might be interested in keeping track of the percent of total daily users who are accessing shared servers from off-campus locations via an Internet connection versus the number of users who access the shared server from a dial in connection, or via the campus network.

Issues

This measure assumes that the server's network operating system administrative tools will allow for the collection of the IP addresses of computers requesting access. Depending on the network operating system of the server, this may or may not be a valid assumption. Unix based servers keep log files of such activity. Users will need to consult with their technical staff.

Data Collection

Institutions could create a batch file of all the IP addresses that access the shared server. A management program could sort through the IP addresses and group those that are on-campus, those that are from commercial internet service providers (i.e. AOL, Compuserv), and those that are temporarily assigned dial-in IP addresses.

Alternatively, the institution could contact its local Internet service providers to determine if they would provide a count of the number of connections, or number of users, accessing the university's IP addresses through their service.

Most server network operating systems include administrative tools that record the IP addresses of machines which request access to it. Users would need to sort these addresses by:

- Access through Internet providers
- Access through dial-in connection
- Access through the campus network.

Data Analysis

With this data, users of the manual could produce the following measures:

$$\frac{access\ to\ shared\ server\ via\ commercial\ provider}{total\ access\ to\ shared\ server}$$

$$\frac{access\ to\ shared\ server\ via\ dial\text{-}in\ connection}{total\ access\ to\ shared\ server}$$

Using these ratios, users of the manual can see over time how users are accessing information or services on the shared server.

NETWORK SERVICES

Online Library Catalog Measures

- Number of remote logins to the online library catalog

- Number of non-remote logins to the online library catalog

- Number of searches made from remote and non-remote terminals

- Cost of online library catalog per remote log-in

- Cost of online library catalog per non-remote log-in

Definition

Online public access catalogs (OPACs) are computerized bibliographic databases of a library's holdings. They may be accessed in the library itself through public access terminals or from remote locations (i.e., outside the library via the campus network or via off-campus telnet). Some schools do not offer remote access to their library's online catalog so some of the measures in this section may be inapplicable.

Issues

- <u>Definitions of OPAC Use</u>. Different institutions may choose to measure different types of OPAC use. Some may measure individual searches while others measure, log-ins, or sessions. A search may be defined as the pursuit of materials related to a specific topic. A log-in may be defined as a connection to the OPAC. A session may be defined as the time between the log-in and the log-off, or the disconnection from the OPAC. Each institution will need to determine what types of use to measure.

- <u>Definition of Remote User</u>. Institutions may wish to consider how best to define the term "remote user" for this measure. There are different types of remote users which can include users not physically in the library but using the campus network from on campus; users who dial-up from either on-campus or off-campus directly to the OPAC; and users who telnet into the campus network and then connect to the OPAC. Depending on the type of connections available at a particular campus, the definition of a "remote user" may be modified.

- <u>Measurement Methods</u>. A serious problem complicates the measurement of traffic into a library's online catalog. Since the hard-wired terminals in a library oftentimes do not require log-in/log-out procedures, measuring OPAC traffic can be difficult. One cannot know when one non-remote user finishes a session and when the next non-remote user begins a session at the same terminal. Four possible, though not ideal, solutions are to

  - require non-remote users to log-in (via their social security number or campus ID number, for example) before each search query;

  - require non-remote users to swipe a digitally-encoded card (e.g., an identification card) through a card reader before each search query;

  - measure the number of searches instead of users as an indicator for traffic. This is a measure of OPAC traffic as opposed to a count of OPAC users. These two measures are not the same: a user count measures people and a search count measures searches. A search count can be misleading as one cannot know whether a small number of users are performing many searches or many users are performing one or two searches;

- record each time a terminal returns to the start screen (either by user command or by timeout procedure) recorded as one user session. This measure should be used as a last resort as there will be errors embedded in it. Specifically, one user can return to the start screen many times during one session. In addition, a user might start a search where the previous user left off, therefore canceling the timeout procedure.

- Cost Categories and Definitions for OPACs. These will need to be identified and defined at each institution to calculate cost components for these measures.

- On-site versus Off-site Searches. Some OPACS restrict search options for remote users. For example, remote users might be users off-campus who telnet or dial-in to the OPAC, or users not in the library itself. In such instances tracking the kind of searches or applications used by on-site versus remote users cannot be compared and should be counted by type of access.

- Responsibility for the OPAC. At some institutions, the OPAC is maintained by library staff. At others, it is managed by the institution's computer center. And at others, the OPAC is managed by both library and computer center staff. Evaluation of the OPAC services may involve determining who, exactly, is responsible for managing the OPAC and coordinating the assessment techniques with the appropriate individuals.

Data Collection

1. Determine an appropriate sampling period. The sampling period should represent a "typical" time of at least one week and preferably two weeks. Do not select a time period that might result in exceptionally heavy or light use.

2. Many automated library systems incorporate library management systems which can be used to record and analyze statistics on OPAC use (e.g., *NOTIS LMS* from Ameritech Library Services, Inc.). When available, use such a system to measure the total number of connections made from remote locations and the total number of searches from remote and non-remote terminals.

3. Calculate the costs of the online catalog by adding together all expenditures (i.e., equipment such as computers and wiring) and all expenses (i.e., support and maintenance). At some schools, this may require the library, computer center and perhaps other departments to account for all costs.

Data Analysis

If any of the four previously-mentioned solutions for measuring OPAC traffic are implemented, comparisons can be made between remote and non-remote users. For instance, one can compute:

$$\frac{total\ number\ of\ remote\ connections}{total\ number\ of\ connections}$$

By subtracting the resulting percentage from 100% one can obtain the percentage of users that are non-remote users. One can also calculate:

$$\frac{cost\ of\ OPAC}{total\ number\ non\text{-}remote\ connections}$$

versus

$$\frac{cost\ of\ OPAC\ and\ remote\ equipment}{total\ number\ of\ remote\ connections}$$

The denominators of these equations can be modified if search counts are used instead of user counts. The first equation would then provide the percentage of searches that are from remote terminals. The second and third equations would show the cost of the OPAC per remote and non-remote search.

Conceivably, it would be possible to measure the number of hits people made using the online library catalog. It might also be interesting to determine, via a transaction log analysis, if people gained access to other information sources after using the library catalog since some online library catalogs provide access to other catalogs, journal article databases, and so on (see Appendix B.4 for an example of such a log). Another measure might be to compare the number of university users versus outside users. The university users might be divided into faculty, students, staff and other categories.

Discussion

A longitudinal analysis of these measures is ideal for tracking OPAC measures over time. Knowing the cost of the OPAC per remote and non-remote connection provides useful information in funding decisions. For example, decisions on whether to put money into buying more non-remote terminals versus offering more remote connections into the OPAC can be made more effectively with the evidence collected from these measures.

There is a growing body of literature related to measuring OPAC use and related OPAC activities. Thorne and Whitlatch (1994) provide an excellent introduction to measuring OPAC use and other variables from a user point-of-view.

Additional Suggestions

The measures (1) number of remote logins to the OPAC, (2) number of non-remote logins to the OPAC, and (3) number of searches made from remote and non-remote terminals can be modified to assess the number of *successful* logins and searches. Thus, instead of measuring only a count of the activities, there would also be an assessment of the degree to which the logins, searches, or sessions, were successful. To use such measures, criteria for "success" would need to be defined, or at the completion of a search or session, the user could be asked with pop-up screens the degree to which they believe the activities to be successful.

Evaluators may wish to track the different types of screens used during a search session to better understand how users use the OPAC. For example, it may be useful to know that the majority of users conduct subject searches rather than author searches. Knowledge of the amount of time spent on particular screens may also be useful as well as the total amount of time typically spent on a search session.

Campus-Wide Information Services

- Total number of visitors to the CWIS

- Total number and/or percentage of faculty/students/staff/others visiting the CWIS

- Frequency of visits from each visitor or group (i.e., faculty, students, staff, etc.)

- Sites visited within the CWIS for each visitor

- Location of visitors after they leave the CWIS

Definition

A campus-wide information service (CWIS) is a Web-based or Gopher-based application that integrates and makes available a range of information services on a campus through a common user interface. The CWIS provides faculty, staff, and students easy access to information that resides on computers both on campus and beyond.

Data Collection

Commercial software exists that makes evaluation of CWIS relatively straightforward. Such software requires first-time visitors to the CWIS to register (i.e., by entering demographic and personal information) before accessing the CWIS. This information is stored in a database along with a log of which Web or Gopher pages the visitor travelled to within the CWIS. Each time a registered visitor accesses the CWIS, the log is updated without the visitor re-registering. If users refuse to register and provide additional information about themselves, their use of the CWIS would still be recorded.

Data Analysis

One of the advantages of using this type of tracking software is that evaluation can be ongoing. Statistics from the measures listed above can be generated from this database for evaluation purposes. The registration process can be customized so that all the information the evaluator wants to obtain can be requested during the registration.

Once the data are collected, the counts and measures described in this section can be calculated automatically for a given period of time. In addition, tables and graphs can also be generated for pictorial representations of CWIS traffic.

Analysis of user demographic information (e.g., campus or non-campus member, type of campus member, age, department affiliation, etc.) versus types of services and resources requested can provide useful information that might aid in the future development of these services.

Discussion

This is one of the few parts of the academic networked environment where technology makes evaluation more straight forward. However, it is important to know that visitors sometimes give false information during the registration process. Therefore, the database must be searched for anomalies. If data appear suspicious, it is advisable to check it against other sources (if possible) or exclude such data from the CWIS evaluation.

A less expensive but also less robust solution to measuring CWIS traffic is to install software that "counts" the number of hits various Web pages receive. This approach has a number of limitations such as the inability to determine who is using what specific pages or counting the number of users as opposed to the number of pages hit. Appendix C contains additional information about using such software.

Additional Suggestions

Counts of CWIS hits and areas on the CWIS that are most frequently visited are important measures of the extent to which the CWIS is used. "Pop up" questionnaires can also be embedded in selected CWIS pages or services to obtain users' assessment of the quality or usefulness of these specific applications.

An example of this technique (as of February, 1996) is the Syracuse Online Web site: <http://www.syracuse.com>. The site's users provide feedback on the quality and usefulness of the site by selecting one of four buttons available on each page: a button with a plus sign for positive comments, a button with a minus sign for criticism, a button with a question mark for questions, and a button with an exclamation mark for other comments.

Distance Learning

- Number of distance learning classes offered in a given semester.

- Distance learning classes as a percentage of all offered classes.

- Number of faculty offering distance learning classes in a given semester via the network.

- Percentage of faculty teaching via distance learning in a given semester via the network.

- Number of students enrolled in distance learning classes in a given semester.

- Percent of all students enrolled in distance learning classes in a given semester.

- Distance learning student grade point average compared to non-distance learning student GPA.

- Unique costs associated with distance learning classes.

Definition

Distance learning classes are defined here as classes that are delivered through the network such that registered students participate in classes from locations distant from the university setting. Distance learning classes may be provided in a number of different formats using a variety of network-based technologies.

Data Collection

1. In the absence of a centralized distance learning office on campus, a primary source of distance learning information would be the individual departments offering such courses. Those departments are in the best position to provide data on specific distance learning course offerings, student enrollments, full time equivalent (FTE) faculty assignments, unique departmental costs associated with distance learning, and student performance measures for the distance learning program.

These unique costs may include additional faculty compensation and additional technology costs (e.g., cameras, 800 numbers). Student performance measures are usually quiz, examination, and final grade reports. Grade point average comparisons can be made between students taking the same courses via different delivery methods: the traditional classroom and via distance learning. Obtaining grade point averages will require consultation with the Registrar's office and/or faculty members. Users of the manual should know in advance that there may be confidentiality issues or academic restrictions on the release of student grades.

2. The Registrar's office may be the best source of information for total campus student enrollments, campus wide full-time equivalent (FTE) faculty assignments, and the total number of offered courses.

Issues

- Definitions. The term "distance learning" and "distance learning course" may vary among institutions. Each institution, or department, will need to define those courses that meet their definition of a "distance learning course." Typically, "distance learning" courses will be those where the student spends the majority of learning time away from the main institution.

- Range of Distance Education Technologies. There are numerous "distance learning" technologies that may be employed uniquely or in combination with others. They range from video tapes, email, and telephone conversations, to interactive satellite systems. These technologies may be provided by individual departments, or through the centralized computer and information technologies group.

- Cost Categories. Definition of specific cost categories to be included in "distance education costs" may need to be developed within each institution. These may include, but are not limited to, additional faculty compensation for teaching in the distance learning program and additional technology costs, either directly budgeted within the department or charged back from a central location. These costs may include network charges for communications circuits, satellite transponder time, miscellaneous items such as studio lighting and tape production equipment, as well as additional expenses for technical help in the production and delivery of distance learning course materials.

Data Analysis

The total number of distance learning courses and the percentage of all classes offered in this manner can be calculated each semester. A trend analysis will show whether there is growth in the number of courses offered in this manner. Similar calculations will show quantities and trends of faculty and student involvement in distance learning.

Comparison of learning competency between students involved in identical courses in "distance" and traditional on-campus learning environments can be done through comparison of scores on identical, or equally comprehensive examinations. A ratio of the average grades of the two groups should be calculated and tracked over time to ascertain the direction of competency in the distance learning program.

A ratio of the total unique costs for distance learning to the number of courses taught and to the enrolled students can be calculated as two separate measures. These measures of cost per course and cost per student can also be tracked over time.

Discussion

Distance learning is a growing trend in the United States and is attracting the non-traditional learner as well as students interested in course variety and flexible scheduling. In addition, the background of distance education students may vary from those typically taking the course on-site. The measure of "success" for distance learning in the academic environment (as well as a range of other issues related to the role of distance education) has been debated and discussed by a number of different authors (e.g., Thorpe, 1988; Franklin, Yoakin, and Warrem, 1995; and Caldor, 1994).

Additional Suggestions

Calculating credit hours generated by distance education and comparing that number to the number of credit hours generated by traditional instruction may be a useful ratio for network administrators to track. In addition, it may be useful to know the departments from which these distance education courses have been generated.

Assessment of student and faculty perception of the quality of distance learning programs can also be accomplished by various qualitative data collection techniques or with the user survey as discussed, respectively, in Parts II and IV of the manual.

SUPPORT SERVICES

Help Desk

- Volume of Requests

- Types of Requests

- Response Time

- Accuracy of Response

- Courtesy of Staff

Definition

The help desk is a user support service provided by a central academic computing group on the campus. This support is usually in the form of answering questions from users regarding hardware, software, applications, or other aspects of the institution's computing services. Three means of help support can be provided: electronic, telephone, and walk-in. Measures can be computed for each of these three services.

Issues

- Range of Help Desk Questions. Requests for information that come to the help services may be inappropriate or not under the jurisdiction of the institution. For example, it may not be the responsibility of the institution to be able to explain to users why a particular Web site in Australia is not operational.

- Training of Help Desk Staff. Assessment of help desk services may wish to take into consideration the range and type of training provided to persons providing these services.

- Distributed Help Desks. Some institutions may have a number of help desk services throughout the campus. A decision will need to be made whether to assess all, some, or only the central or main help desk.

Data Collection

1. Determine which of the three types of help support you wish to measure (i.e., electronic, telephone, or walk-in), or if you wish to measure all three.

2. Select an appropriate sampling period to monitor the help requests and responses. The sampling period should represent a "typical" time of at least one week and preferably two weeks. Do not select a time period that might result in exceptionally heavy or light requests from users.

3. Determine the type of help desk activities to be counted. For example, requests could be categorized as how-to questions, hardware questions, installation questions, administrative questions, questions regarding specific software applications, etc.

Approach 1: Unobtrusive Testing (for Response Time, Accuracy of Response, and Courtesy of Staff only)

Users of the manual can develop a list of "typical" help desk questions and validates these questions prior to administering them by asking help desk employees (typically at a different location) to review them. Then the evaluator has proxies submit these questions electronically, via the telephone, or in person to the help desk. A record is maintained by the proxies that lists the question asked, time asked, the response received, follow-up by the help desk staff, and the time elapsed before a response was received.

Additional information, such as an assessment of the accuracy of the information and courtesy of the help desk respondent may be collected. A record is maintained by the proxies that lists the answers received, and the courtesy of the help desk staff while answering the query. Appendix B.5 is an example of a form which could be used for this approach.

Approach 2: Transaction Log

In this approach, academic computing personnel document all help desk transactions either electronically for online and telephone requests, or by maintaining a written log of the in-person requests. Staff will first need to identify the appropriate types of categories to describe help desk activities. A transaction log is used to summarize and record the nature of the requests. Appendix B includes an example of such a log.

In this procedure, the staff at the help desk receive a training session on how to complete the transaction log. The transaction log is pretested first to make certain that all appropriate categories and options are represented on the log. A training session for help desk staff on how to complete the log should improve the quality of the data they report on the log. All employees staffing the help desk complete the log immediately after each specific transaction is completed.

Data Analysis

The transaction log, maintained either manually or by management software, provides an accounting of the volume of requests and the types of requests. Both the unobtrusive and the transaction log techniques produce logs indicating:

- When the question was asked

- When the question was answered

- Additional information as included/requested on the log.

Users of the manual can compute the time elapsed between when the question was asked and when the question was answered, including any time for follow-up and referral. A question is considered answered when the help desk indicates there is no further action it can take with the question or does not respond after two weeks. Manual users can also determine the percentage of instances in which there was no answer provided.

The unobtrusive testing will result in additional measures such as:

- Accuracy of the information

- Nature and type of referrals

- Courtesy of staff.

The "correct answer fill rate" is the percentage of questions asked that are answered correctly by the help desk. This measure can be computed if correct answers to the questions posed by the evaluators are known and agreed upon in advance of the data collection.

The proxies can assess the courtesy (or other skills/attitudes) of the help desk responses using a Likert scale of 1 = very courteous to 5 = very discourteous. These scores can be averaged for the entire test period or for particular time periods to calculate scores that suggest an average level of courtesy for help desk responses (see also Part IV for user survey questions that address this topic).

Discussion

Users requesting help require quick and accurate responses to their queries. Unobtrusive testing will provide data to determine response time for as well as the accuracy of the response. Each institution should determine the response time that they consider acceptable for a help request. Each institution should also determine the acceptable error rate to assess the efficacy of the service at the help desk.

Additional Suggestions

To determine the accuracy and courtesy of responses, typical questions should be developed before the sample period to which the answers are known by the evaluators. Additionally, measures can be developed to determine what types of questions people ask and how many people seek certain kinds of help (online, phone, person). The latter can only be done through the log, not through unobtrusive testing.

An analysis of the kinds of questions asked can point to deficiencies in services provided and can provide support for resource requests to remedy those deficiencies. The analysis can also inform network administrators about frequently asked questions (FAQs) for which answers might be automated or found elsewhere.

The ratio of help staff hours provided to number of transactions may be helpful for the institution when rating their help desk. If the response time is below acceptable standards, the problem may be inadequate staffing. The number of staff hours may be linked to the response time, accuracy, and courtesy of the staff. Such data could be useful in justifying or obtaining resources, and they may also be useful in benchmarking (see Part II) by identifying those individuals that provide "outstanding" help services and employing their level of service as goals for the overall department or unit.

If there are multiple help services across the institution or in various departments, it may be useful to assess these various services and compare the volume and type of requests and quality of services provided from each location.

Network Repair and Services

- Response time

- Accuracy of Response

- Courtesy of Staff

Definition

Network repair and services can be assessed in terms of the time between an initial request and the time when that request is fulfilled; the accuracy or success of the response provided by the unit; and the courtesy of the staff in responding to the request.

Introduction

In addition to providing help desk assistance by answering users' questions, the centralized academic computing group also provides physical network services including installation, moves, and changes of network connections and equipment, as well as repair and maintenance of user-based equipment. The normal sequence of activity follows a user request for service, a service commitment, the physical work component, and follow-up to insure user satisfaction. Each of these functions can be measured and compared against benchmarks to assess performance.

Data Collection

1. Transaction logs can be maintained to include the times of each initial request and follow-up action, the intermediate steps taken, and the final time and resolution of the request. Appendix B.6 provides a sample log that might be adapted for use in this situation.

2. Those personnel on the academic computing staff who answer such requests should receive a training session in transaction log preparation and maintenance.

3. Select an appropriate sampling period to monitor and track the requests for service and the associated responses. This sampling period should represent a typical time of at least two weeks and preferably four weeks. Do not select a time period that might result in exceptionally heavy or light service requests from the user community.

4. During the logging process, academic computing personnel document all requests for service either electronically or by maintaining a written log. The log contains specific information, entered at the time of request, concerning the user, the request, and a commitment time provided by the academic computing department. It also contains information about the service activity itself and the actual service completion date. The final data entry is a call-back confirmation to the user ascertaining satisfaction that the work has been completed.

5. After providing the service, staff survey the requestor to determine the degree to which the person is satisfied with the response or accuracy or the response as well as assessing the courtesy to the staff with which the person encountered. The survey might be administered electronically, by phone, or via mail in a print format.

Data Analysis

The transaction log produces data for analysis in the following areas:

1. Time interval between service request and call back verification of completion.

2. Information on intermediate activities that may have affected that time interval in an unexpected manner. Such factors may include delays in obtaining the necessary equipment, inability to access the customer location at the scheduled time, or missed communication between the customer and the staff concerning the request.

3. If benchmarks have been established, each transaction log entry is then compared against the corresponding benchmark and labeled as a "satisfactory" or "less than satisfactory" completion. Within each category of service, a ratio of satisfactory completions to total requests can be computed.

4. The call-back verification also provides an opportunity to elicit data from the customer in terms of satisfaction with the service and an assessment of the courtesy of the staff.

Discussion

Each institution will need to establish response times that they consider acceptable in the various categories of service requests. It is recognized that installation and repair activities are all unique and vary in the amount of work required. However, experience and benchmarking will provide targets for service personnel to meet. The ratio of completions meeting those targets to total requests should be on an upward trend and comparable to institutions following similar measurement plans.

Additional Suggestions

The analysis of the transaction logs can provide a range of information to network decision makers regarding the degree to which appropriate intermediate steps were taken and the appropriateness of the time taken for each of these steps. Process analysis of the steps may identify better or more efficient means to respond to the requests of the customers.

Network officials may also want to include cost information on the transaction log to obtain estimates of staff time, equipment costs, and other costs related to responding to a particular request. Some institutions provide repair services, for example, at no cost, at a fixed rate cost for a particular service, or on an at-cost basis. The transaction log can provide a more meaningful way to assess actual charges for these services.

From experience with the various categories of request, or based on benchmarks obtained from other institutions, "normal" service intervals might be established for each category. These categories could include, but are not limited to: new network connections, hardware installation, software installation, and workstation repair.

Availability of Networked Resources

In Classrooms

- Percentage of classrooms with at least one computer

- Percentage of classrooms with LCD or other type of projector display for computing/networked services or resources

- Percentage of classrooms that have access to the campus network

- Average number of computers per networked classroom

- Average number of network connections per networked classroom

- Percentage of networked classrooms with LCD displays

Other

- Percentage of faculty offices connected to the campus network

- Percentage of administrative offices connected to the campus network

- Percentage of student dorm rooms connected to the campus network

Definition

These indicators describe the capacity of the institution to support electronic teaching in college classrooms and other locations. A networked classroom, office or dorm room is defined as one that has a hard-wired connection to the campus network. LCD or projector displays and computers are those that are assigned permanently to a particular classroom and reside in that classroom.

Issues

- Definitions. Institutions may require additional definitional detail for "classrooms," "computers," "networked classrooms," "network access," and "LCD displays and projectors." Calculating these measures accurately requires that what is counted as a "networked classroom" in one building is the same as that in another building.

- Inventory of classrooms, offices, and dorms. A central listing of classrooms and how they are equipped, may need to be developed and maintained. Such a file may be part of a MIS of a particular administrative unit or may have to be created.

- Unofficial Classrooms. On some campuses there are a number of "unofficial" classrooms, that is, rooms that are used by departments for teaching purposes that are officially "not known" to central classroom scheduling and management. An attempt should be made to identify such facilities and include them in these measures.

- Primary Purpose of Instructional Technology. The number of classrooms, networked connections, computers, and LCD or project displays are counted in the context of *capacity to support instruction*. Thus, it may be necessary to determine if a particular "room with computing facilities" has the primary purpose of supporting instruction rather than some other purpose in calculating these measures.

Data Collection

Users of the manual will have to consult individuals in units such as their campus' Property Coordinator in their Property Accounting Office, Instructional Support Services, Classroom Scheduling, Registrar, or Computer Center and Telecommunications Office to obtain a count of how many computers, connections, and LCD displays are in which classrooms, offices, and dorms. Who specifically should be contacted will depend on individual academic institutions.

Data Analysis

1. Calculating the percentage of all classrooms that have at least one computer is done by (1) determining the total number of classrooms, and (2) identifying which of those classrooms have at least one computer dedicated, in residence, in that classroom.

$$\frac{\textit{Classrooms with at least one computer}}{\textit{Total number of classrooms}}$$

2. Calculating the percentage of all classrooms that have LCD or projector displays is accomplished by identifying the number of classrooms that have at least one LCD or projector display in residence in those classrooms.

$$\frac{\textit{Classrooms with at least one LCD or projector display}}{\textit{Total number of classrooms}}$$

3. Calculating the number of classrooms, offices, or dorm rooms that have at least one hard-wired network connection is accomplished by identifying the total number of classrooms, offices, or dorm rooms with such network access.

$$\frac{\textit{Networked classrooms (offices or dorm rooms)}}{\textit{Total number of classrooms (offices or dorm rooms)}}$$

4. To determine the average number of computers per networked classroom, users of the manual should obtain the total number of computers in all networked classrooms and divide that figure by the number of networked classrooms.

$$\frac{\textit{Total number of computers in networked classrooms}}{\textit{Total number of networked classrooms}}$$

5. To determine the average number of network connections per networked classroom, evaluators should obtain the total number of network connections in all networked classrooms and divide that figure by the number of networked classrooms.

$$\frac{\textit{Total number of network connections in networked classrooms}}{\textit{Total number of networked classrooms}}$$

6. A final calculation can produce the percentage of networked classrooms that have at least one LCD or projector display in residence in that classroom. This can be determined by dividing the total number of networked classrooms that have LCD displays by the total number of networked classrooms.

$$\frac{\textit{Total number of networked classrooms with at least one LCD or projector display}}{\textit{Total number of networked classrooms}}$$

Discussion

Users of the manual may wish to use only some of these indicators. For example, some academic institutions provide their incoming freshmen with laptop computers that the students bring to class and plug into a network connection. In such cases, the number of computers per classroom is irrelevant.

Although some of the indicators are calculated as averages, some evaluators may wish to calculate a measure of variability (i.e., standard deviation). Such a calculation will let users of the manual know if networking resources are distributed equally among classrooms, offices, or dorm rooms or if a minority of classrooms, offices, and dorm rooms have many resources and a majority have few. Many statistical software programs and spreadsheet programs can accomplish the task of calculating standard deviation.

Additional Suggestions

There are a range of options that institutions might employ when measuring the availability of networked resources. For example, "networked classrooms" might be defined to include any classroom with a telephone jack rather than only hardwired to the network. In addition, some institutions may find *counts* of the total number of networked classrooms or counts of the number of computers available for instruction in a classroom adequate indicators of capacity to support electronic instruction.

It may also be interesting to know which departments on campus have the most and the least computing and networking resources for instructional purposes. In such instances it may be useful to compute these measures by department or other academic unit.

Availability of networked resources among students can be affected by the number of students who have purchased their own computers and the degree to which the institution provides dial-in access to the network. A count of the number of students who own their own computer provides additional information about availability to network services and penetration of computer ownership among students.

Depending on the academic institution, penetration rates for other types of users' access to the network may also be of interest. For example, penetration rates for administrative staff, graduate students, etc., may be important to track over time. Penetration rates for faculty by academic units may also be a useful analysis to determine which units have better network access.

In addition to considering penetration rates for other user types, it may be of interest to track penetration rates in the context of different types of network access. For example penetration rates for on campus faculty in terms of direct network access versus dial-up access could be a useful measure.

Lastly, many of the measures in this section can be modified to assess the availability of networked resources in laboratories. In such instances, it will be necessary to define and differentiate between classrooms and labs.

Network Support Staff

· Ratio of support staff to users

· Ratio of support staff to active users

Definition

The ratio of FTE central campus support staff to the total number of network users and active users compares the number of computing support staff available to assist network "users." This measure provides an indicator of the number of users supported by one central campus support staff.

Issues

- Definition. The term "support staff" may vary from and within institutions. One approach is to include as "support staff" those personnel who have as their *primary responsibility* to administer, develop, maintain, repair, and assist users in using the campus network.

- Use in a Distributed Environment. In a highly distributed networking environment these measures may be more appropriate for individual departments or academic units where the unit has its own support staff and there is an identifiable number of users linked to that academic unit.

Data Collection

1. Determine the CNU and CANU (see p. 23).

2. Determine the number of FTE central campus networking support staff. Central campus support staff is defined as the number of full time equivalents who have responsibility for the management, implementation, development, repair, and provision of user support for the campus network (as opposed to departmental or college computing).

Data Analysis

The data collection should result in the computation of two percentages:

$$\frac{CNU}{Number\ of\ FTE\ Support\ Staff}$$

$$\frac{CANU}{Number\ of\ FTE\ Support\ Staff}$$

For example, for measure number two, the institution might determine that there are 150 active network users for each full-time equivalent support staff.

Discussion

Every institution will need to determine an "acceptable" ratio. While some institutions might make the assumption that a high ratio of support staff to users is more appropriate than a lower ratio, others may not. It is presumably easier to obtain network support if there are more people available to provide it. For users, the ratio itself may be less important than the speed with which support is provided and the accuracy or effectiveness of that support. The ratio may be most valuable when used in combination with other measures such as help desk response time.

No assumptions, however, can be made regarding the quality of the support provided. This measure provides an indicator of available support for active users and users. As assessment of the quality of that support is provided elsewhere in this section and may also be calculated by use of qualitative techniques (Part II) or via the user survey (Par IV).

Additional Suggestions

The ratios can be calculated for different types of users (e.g., faculty, staff, students, etc.) if the campus network is able to identify different user groups by email account name. The measures can also be calculated for different types of support staff, e.g., the faculty support group, the technical support group, etc., if support services are organized along such lines.

The ratios can be calculated for every semester and comparisons can be made among them over time. Longitudinal assessment is a valuable tool for tracking changes in these ratios.

These measures are more useful when they are applied in conjunction with a range of user satisfaction measures. Surveys and other assessments of the degree to which users and active users are "satisfied" with the operation and support of the network suggest the degree to which the support-to-user ratios are appropriate for a particular campus networking environment.

Departmental support staff are not included in this measure because they do not provide campus-wide support. If an institution has access to data on the number of networking support staff in individual academic departments or units, it might want to include them as part of overall networking support staff.

If the data are available, ratios may also be calculated for central networking support staff to all users or active users versus ratios for individual departments or academic units to their particular users. In such cases, comparing the ratios between departmental support for local users versus ratios for campus-wide support for all users could provide very useful information regarding overall institutional networking support.

Network Training

- Number of users participating in training

- Number of users seeking training

- Annual training hours received

- Number of training activities offered

- Ratio of application-specific training to available applications

- Training expenditures as a percentage of total IT expenditures

Definition

A training activity is a formal class or other activity provided by computing services which is designed to teach users about one or more computer applications. An application is a software package. Some institutions may wish to modify this definition of a training activity to include a range of training activities such as seminars or other educational activities offered by computing services.

Training support can increase the likelihood that graduates from an institution will be technologically literate, can enable faculty to better use technology in their teaching and research, and can facilitate more efficient administrative functioning at an institution. Overall, network training enhances the academic community's ability to effectively use networking resources, which is an important factor in assessing the quality of an institution's networked environment.

Issues

- Defining Training Experience. A determination of what constitutes a "training experience" will need to be agreed upon prior to calculat-

ing these measures. To some degree this may be a somewhat arbitrary listing of activities on campus that will be counted as "training."

- Multiple Training Techniques. Users of the manual should also be aware that, increasingly, there are other techniques and resources available to support training and instruction: tutorials, videos, demonstrations, discussion lists, etc. Depending on the techniques used at a specific institution, these may also be measured and analyzed.

- Training Costs. Defining training cost categories as a part of total IT expenditures will need to be resolved by each institution. Characteristic network training costs include staff time, instructional materials, facility rental or construction, equipment and software. Costs will vary depending on whether an institution has a centralized training program, departmental based training, training offered by the library, or a combination of these.

Data Collection

1. Determine the sample time period for each of the above measures (e.g., a semester, an academic year, or summer).

2. Maintain a database that minimally contains the following:

   - the number of training activities given during the sample period and the applications that they support.

   - the number of people attending the training during the sample period and the amount of training time (in hours) received by those individuals.

   - a list of all the applications available through the network.

   - the number of people seeking instruction.

The training activity costs and standard cost categories can then be compared over time. Appendix B.7 offers an example of a data collection form for developing such a database.

Data Analysis

The data collection should result in the computation of the following:

1. Number of users participating in training activities

2. Total training hours received by participants

3. Number of users turned away due to training activities being full

4. Number of different applications-specific training activities offered

5. Training support for networked applications

$$\frac{\textit{Number of different applications-specific training activities offered}}{\textit{Number of different applications provided through the network}}$$

6. Training costs as a percentage of total IT expenditures

$$\frac{\textit{Training activity costs}}{\textit{Total IT expenditures}}$$

Discussion

Number 1 and 2 above are frequency counts of training activities and hours of training received. The third item is a percentage that shows the extent to which the applications offered through the network are covered by training activities. In theory it should be possible for users to obtain training for any application that is offered. In practice it might be that not all applications are supported. Every institution will have to determine an "acceptable" ratio of support.

A count of training hours received by participants is more descriptive of actual training efforts than a count of participants since some training times will likely vary.

Training may be outsourced, particularly for a staff client group. The advantage of outsourcing is that a group of specialists can be tapped regularly to provide training for a diverse range of applications. Institutional staff constraints may reduce the availability of in-house training for certain applications. On the other hand, outsourcing can have hidden costs, if for example, the institution handles the advertising, registration, and billing for vendor ser-

vices. Institutions will have to evaluate how training funds are best utilized in these situations.

Additional Suggestions

Members of the academic community have a variable knowledge level, ranging from minimal to expert, of how to use networked resources. Furthermore, within varying skill levels, training needs also vary across the basic client groups that comprise the academic community; students, staff, and faculty. Typically, students want access to introductory workshops and selected advanced workshops, while faculty desire more customized training, and staff require in-depth training for a different set of applications. The data can be analyzed for different types of clients and sample period results can be compared over time.

These measures yield particularly useful data when they are analyzed in conjunction with a range of user satisfaction measures. For example, simply counting the number of training activities offered and the number of attendees at the various types of training activities would provide more complete assessment information for evaluators if linked to the user survey (Part IV) or qualitative data (Part II) that assesses the quality of workshops.

Below is an additional measure that can assist decision makers in monitoring the costs of training:

$$\frac{\textit{Amount of training expenditures}}{\textit{CNU or CANU (network users or active network users)}}$$

Data collected from this measure can assess the levels of training offered to different groups and can be used to compare application costs. This information can be combined with the number of users participating in training activities to make informed decisions about which applications to support with training.

Network Documentation Available to Users

- Count of print-based documentation available

- Count of electronic-based documentation available

- Usefulness of documentation

- Annual cost of documentation

Definition

Network documentation consists of help guides made publicly available by the institution, either in print or via electronic means, that provide information to assist the user with applications available through the network. Such guides might be produced locally or purchased from other providers in print or electronic formats. Guides can also provide background information concerning computers and their use on the network.

Issues

- Distributed Environments. In calculating these measures, the institution will have to decide if it will include only the documentation from the central computing facility or if it will include the documentation from individual departments or other units on campus. Conceivably, different schools or departments could produce their own help guides for their target populations.

- Embedded "Guides." Unix operating systems often come with a limited number of pre-written "man" or manual pages to which institutions may add customized information. The institution will have to decide if it wishes to parse out those pages created locally from the pages included with the original operating system.

Data Collection: Print Documentation

1. Establish a sample period of a typical two-week interval during the academic year. Collect all information for these counts during this interval.

2. Determine the number of print-based help guides available. Some institutions maintain a central file of network documentation. In such instances, simply count the number of guides available. Also make certain that all guides offered are available. For instance, if guides are obtained from a central file, make sure that none are momentarily "sold out."

3. If the institution wishes to include help guides produced by other campus groups, it will have to contact each school or department to obtain copies of their material.

4. Determine the usefulness of the documentation by surveying users, including return questionnaires as part of the documentation, or by conducting focus group sessions or using other data collection techniques (see Parts II and IV).

Data Collection: Electronic Help Guides

1. Establish a sample period of a typical two-week interval during the academic year. Collect all information for these counts during this interval.

2. Determine the number of electronic help guides available. Develop a typology of documentation available. Electronic documentation or help guides may consist of any or all of the following: local newsgroups where users discuss tips for using an application, web pages describing how to use a particular application, web interfaces providing access to a help desk search engine for a questions and answers database, Unix tutoring programs, or many other kinds of electronic resources.

   If the institution wishes to include electronic sources developed by other campus groups, it will have to contact those groups regarding collecting samples of the information.

3. Determine the extent of use of the electronic documentation and the usefulness of these services.

   In the case of campus newsgroups that discuss tips for using an application, the investigator may wish to determine to what extent users take advantage of the newsgroup. To do this, the investigator could count the number of new messages posted to the newsgroup during the sampling period, or the number of different users who post messages.

   To measure the benefits of the campus newsgroup, the investigator could use an unobtrusive testing technique and post a series of predetermined questions to the newsgroup and calculate how long it took to receive a correct answer.

   To determine the extent of use for the question and answer database, the investigator could install software to count the number of hits on the web page. Several packages are available. Some cannot discriminate the number of different users who access the database. Other software packages ask users to log on using a user I.D. These systems can provide a fairly accurate count of how many different users took advantage of the question and answer service.

To measure the usefulness of a Web-based search engine for a help desk question and answer database, users of the manual could use an unobtrusive testing technique and attempt to use the database to answer a series of pre-determined questions.

Data Collection: Annual Cost of Documentation

To calculate this measure, users of the manual need to maintain an annual record that identifies for each guide or other type of documentation the costs associated with the production of that guide. Typical costs associated with the production of guides and documentation may include:

- Staff time to design, write, test, and rewrite the guide

- Editors who review the guide

- Software or other support necessary to produce the guide

- Material such as paper, binders, etc.

- Duplication

- Distribution

Each institution will need to determine which costs will be included to define "Annual Cost of Documentation." In addition, the institution will need to determine if these costs will be calculated campus-wide, for central networking services, or for individual campus units or departments. Maintaining a central database of documentation information (including cost data) simplifies the calculation of this measure.

Data Analysis

In situations where the identical guide is offered in two formats, paper and electronic, a distinction should be made to indicate that duplication exists.

The data should provide an overall count of the number and type of help guides available for each

application offered by the network, as well as the number of users who use an electronic help guide or database. An unobtrusive test of the help listservs should provide the average amount of time needed to get a correct answer to a pre-determined question. An unobtrusive test of the question and answer database should yield a percent of questions answered correctly by the database.

Discussion

These measures give some indication as to the availability of network documentation and help guides available for users, the number of users using electronic help guides, and the usefulness of the electronic and print-based help guides.

Users of the manual who unobtrusively test the time required for a correct answer to a predetermined question posted on a help newsgroup may decide to increase or decrease the number of support staff required to read the newsgroup in response to the results.

The number of new posts to a newsgroup cannot really provide an accurate count of the total number of users reading the newsgroup, because many users may be "lurking" - reading the posted information, but not posting any questions or answers of their own. It may be possible, however, to determine the number of individuals that are subscribed to these newsgroups and track the growth and activity of the newsgroup over time.

Depending on the percentage of questions answered correctly by a question and answer database, and the institution's own goals, the institution may decide to devote more or fewer resources to updating the database. The institution should be certain to include a user feedback mechanism in the Web interface for the database so that users can note what questions they could not find answers to, or what aspects of the database they found confusing. Depending on the number of different users accessing the database, the institution may choose to increase or decrease publicity or training for using the database.

Additional Suggestions

Combining this count with information from a user survey or a qualitative data collection method could provide a more accurate indication of the quality or usefulness of the guides than just using the quantitative measures outlined above. The authors suggest that institutions use this measure in tandem with the section of the user survey which addresses help guides and with a qualitative data collection method such as a focus group.

Some questions that a user survey or a focus group can answer include: How useful are the help guides? Can the users easily read and understand the help guides? Do help guides exist for all applications that users require? Can the users access the help guides when they need them? Do the newsgroups give good advice about how to solve problems? How useful is the Web-based question and answer database?

Users of the manual may include assessment forms as part of the guides. In either a print or electronic format, users have a method to provide feedback to the developers of the guides. Such data can be used as part of an ongoing process to monitor and assess the usefulness of the guides.

PART IV: USER SURVEY

Introduction

Any evaluation of network technologies and services will benefit from an evaluation from the users' perspective. Some academic institutions, such as Indiana University, have successfully administered user surveys assessing the networked environment on a regular basis and have a powerful data base of longitudinal information that assists in network planning and development. When used in addition to the data collection techniques and the measures outlined previously in the manual, a user survey can broaden the scope and quality of data collection.

In this manual, users are defined as all members of the authorized service community. This group includes students, faculty, staff, and others. Users of the manual should know who the users are, what their needs and expectations are, and whether those needs and expectations are being met. Users' responses to questions about how they use network services and their degree of satisfaction with those services can be analyzed as part of the evaluation process. The user survey included in this section can be administered to both known users and authorized users who do not use the campus network.

The development of a survey that fits the needs of all institutions of higher education is an impossible task. Thus, the guidelines and model survey included in this section offer an approach that users of the manual can customize and refine to fit the needs of their particular institution. The model survey offered in this section is a *beginning basis* from which a short and effective survey can be developed.

Designers of network user surveys may benefit by reviewing surveys that have been developed by other organizations and institutions. Increasingly, one can locate such surveys and results on various academic Web pages. Appendix D describes three national survey efforts that provide a good introduction to the types of survey questions and techniques that might be modified for use in local settings.

Purpose of Model User Survey

The primary purpose of the user survey is to obtain a profile of the people who use the network, to learn how they use it, to assess their satisfaction with it, and to find out how campus networks are affecting users. The following questions can be answered by this user survey:

- Who are the users?

- When do they use the network?

- How do they access the network?

- How do they use the network, i.e., what types of activities do they engage in while using it?

- How satisfied are they with the network?

- How useful do they believe the network is?

- What do they think is successful about the network and what needs to be improved?

- What impact is the network having on various aspects of the users' activities?

Answers to these questions, especially when combined with other techniques described in Part II and III can provide very useful information for decision makers as they plan and develop the network.

Issues Related to Method

Errors, Reliability, and Validity. There is always some amount of error in data collection. Random errors are unpredictable but can be reduced by selecting a larger and more representative sample (Fink, 1995). Errors can occur if the survey does not accurately measure what it proposes to measure. The objective is to produce results which are as reliable (reproducible) and valid (accurate) as possible. In some instances specific, reliable measures can reduce the richness in meaning (validity) of general concepts. Because of this, Babbie (1992) recommends using several different approaches that will highlight different aspects of the concept under investigation.

Bias. Survey data accuracy can be diminished by social desirability bias, i.e., the tendency of respondents to give answers to questions "in a way that conforms to dominant belief patterns among groups to which the respondent feels some identification or allegiance" (Dillman, 1978, p. 62). The surveyed

users may give answers that make them look good but are not representative of what they really think or feel. One way to avoid bias is by constructing questions that are neutral and avoid asking people to think that there is a "right way" and a "wrong way" to answer (Babbie, 1992).

Who Can Administer the Survey. This survey can be administered by a central network services office, by distributed computing departments, or by libraries, depending upon the organizational structure of networking services, the objectives for doing the survey, the budget, and the procedures and format used to administer it. Changes and modifications in specific questions included in the model survey may depend on the unit identified to be most appropriate to administer the survey.

Choice of Survey Administration Method

In general, there are two types of survey methods: self-administered and interviews. Each has advantages and disadvantages, but, assuming that most institutions have limited resources for conducting an evaluation, a self-administered mail survey may be the most feasible choice.

Self-administered surveys. This type of survey uses questionnaires which the respondents complete themselves. The most commonly used medium of the questionnaire is paper, and responses are handwritten. Computerized forms of questionnaires are likely to become more prevalent and will offer several important advantages: data do not have to be re-keyed for subsequent analysis, responses may be more complete, and the response rate may be higher. Completed surveys should be anonymous unless respondents are informed in advance to the contrary.

Self-administered surveys can be implemented in a number of ways ranging from supervised to unsupervised (Fink, 1995):

- *One-to-one supervision:* An interviewer and a respondent are alone together. The administrator is available to answer questions about the survey, but confidentiality is injured. This is a very labor-intensive method and would not be cost effective for large sample groups.

- *Group supervision:* Questionnaires are given to people who are together in large groups in a classroom or auditorium. The administrator is available to answer questions and monitor the completion of the survey. A disadvantage of this method is that it is difficult to organize and schedule large groups who are willing to complete a survey.

- *Semi-supervised:* Questionnaires are handed to people along with verbal and written instructions, but they are not closely supervised when they complete the survey. Semisupervised surveys could be passed out to people standing in lines or when they are entering or exiting buildings. Although this kind of survey is fairly inexpensive, it is difficult to achieve a representative sample and to ensure that the surveys will be completed and returned.

- *Unsupervised:* Questionnaires, along with a cover letter and instructions, are mailed to people who assume the responsibility for completing and returning the survey. This is the least expensive method of administering surveys, and can be sent to a representative sample of the user community, making the likelihood of receiving a representative response possible. Unfortunately, the administrator has no control over who responds.

Each of the above approaches have their own strengths and weaknesses. Time and financial constraints will also affect the decision as to which approach might be better for a given situation.

Interviews. Survey interviews are conversations; an interviewer asks a respondent a series of prepared questions. Interviewing is more expensive to conduct than a self-administered survey, but the quality of the response can be enhanced by the interviewer who can interact effectively with respondents to explain questions, probe for further information, and obtain complete responses. This method allows for the most control of responses, and does not have to rely on a person's motivation to complete and return the survey. There are two major types of interviews (Fink, 1995):

- *In-person interviews* are similar to one-on-one self-administered surveys, because they are conducted with individuals and the interviewer asks questions and records the responses. Al-

though this method has high costs for hiring, training, and deploying interviewers, it can produce better response rates.

- *Telephone interviews* are conducted by interviewers who call people who are either on a predetermined list or randomly selected. Costs can still be significant as personnel and telephone facilities must be used.

It may also be beneficial to combine these approaches and conduct some interviews in person while other interviews are conducted via the telephone. By deleting and adding questions, and creating an interview script, this mail survey could be modified for use as an interview instrument.

Electronic Questionnaires

The electronic questionnaire can be thought of as a logical extension of the more commonly used face-to-face and mail-in varieties. Since the survey involves the use of, and perceptions of, the electronic network, the on-line questionnaire seems a natural application. An electronic survey will be most effective when the purpose is to focus more clearly on a specific aspect of the academic network involving knowledgeable network users. There are, however, some issues to consider in using an electronic survey:

- Respondents to an on-line questionnaire will likely be those with more than minimal networking skills and their attitudes may be biased in favor of networking. This technique should therefore be used to clarify certain "user" issues and not to address the fundamental questions of whether individuals use the network, how much they use it, or whether they like it or not.

- The audience must be properly selected to elicit responses directed at clearly defined issues. They should be current network users, as determined through pre-screening, and should comprise a pool that will offer a range of responses.

- The questions should be thoughtfully selected to focus on specific issues. The aim could be to focus, for example, could be on assessment of applications, data base quality, and/or training requirements.

- The results must be carefully analyzed to detect bias or a lack of variability. Results that do not show a range of response may indicate an improperly designed study. Changes in the participant selection and questions may be required to improve the validity of the results.

Nonetheless, use of an electronic survey for targeted users may be a more efficient means to administer the survey.

The electronic survey can be used to elicit information about the effectiveness, efficiency, and impacts of academic networks if carefully and skillfully administered. One important application is to focus on specific issues with a carefully chosen target population. An example would be an electronic questionnaire administered to law school students to assess the perceived quality of resources on the network, as compared to in-house resources, and the ease and accessibility of those networked resources. It may be especially useful to compare results from the electronic survey to data collection using other techniques.

Getting Ready

Obtain approval. In order to administer a survey, approval should be obtained from the parent organization. Many college administrations require that proposals for research that will use people as subjects be reviewed in advance. The purpose of the review is to protect the welfare and confidentiality of the participants, i.e., the user survey respondents. Before proceeding with the survey, contact the appropriate office on campus. Obtaining approval may take several weeks or months, so plan accordingly.

Determine a budget. There are costs associated with implementing a survey. Personnel time, equipment, facilities rental, printing, postage, and other costs should be anticipated and budgeted in advance of administering the survey. The costs incurred will depend upon the method of survey chosen. Self-administered surveys are the least expensive compared to in-person and telephone interviews. Questionnaires administered by mail cost about 50% less than those administered by telephone and 75% less than those administered by personal interview (Fink, 1995).

Select a survey administration method. This is dependent on variables previously discussed, such as funding and the objectives of the surveys. Never-

theless, the approach must be determined and specific tasks to implement it should be identified.

Inform people. It will be easier to have people cooperate with the evaluation if they are told about the survey and why it is being done. The more they know about and understand the purpose of the survey and its procedures, the more smoothly the process will unfold. The entire networked computing services staff should be informed about the survey, preferably by the person in charge of the evaluation. One benefit of disclosure is that the staff will know how to answer questions about the survey or will be ready to refer questions to the appropriate person. Second, personnel may feel threatened by the survey, fearing that, as individuals, they will be targets for evaluation. If they understand that the purpose of the survey is not to scrutinize individuals, their fears can be alleviated. Third, the staff may have suggestions about how to improve the survey process (Van House, et al., 1990). Results of the survey should be made available to respondents in a timely fashion.

Set a timeline. All activities related to preparation and administration of the survey as well as analysis of the data collected should be plotted on a timeline. Specific deadlines for completion of each activity should be established. Key steps to consider include:

- Step 1: clarify the survey objectives.

- Step 2: identify the target group and select a representative sample.

- Step 3: modify/revise the survey, pretest, and prepare final version.

- Step 4: print and copy the survey.

- Step 5: distribute the survey.

- Step 3: send reminders, collect the data.

- Step 4: analyze the data and prepare reports.

Modify the user survey. The user survey provided in this manual will likely need some modification to fit an organization's particular needs. The survey should be used as a template and it should be customized as necessary. For example, if the institution does not have a graduate program, then question #1 can be modified to exclude "graduate student" as a choice. Questions that relate more closely to the characteristics of your user groups, networked computing's structure and services, and the goals and objectives of the evaluation may be added.

Pretest the survey. Once the survey is modified, it is important that it is pretested with a small group of individuals similar in composition to those who will actually receive the survey. The pretest group should read the survey and, in addition to completing it, provide feedback about reading comprehension problems, typographical errors, design layout and flow difficulties. Pretesting will provide an opportunity to gauge how long the survey will take to complete and can identify other problems that may need to be considered and corrected before the final version is printed and distributed.

Administering the Survey

Distribute questionnaires. Ideally, all members of the authorized service community should be surveyed. It is advisable to select a random sample that is of sufficient size to minimize the standard error (i.e., the difference between sample statistics and their corresponding population parameters). In this way evaluators can be more confident that the sample is representative of the population of interest. Different groups of users, students, faculty, staff, and others, can be surveyed. Existing guidelines should be consulted for determining sample size and selecting random samples (Babbie, 1992).

Once a target sample group is identified, and the final set of questions are prepared, it is time to administer the survey. A cover letter should be included with a self-administered mail survey that describes the importance of the survey and the need for the user to respond. Be sure to include a deadline and return address for the completed surveys.

Collect the responses. A good to very good response rate ranges from 50-70%. Thus, it will almost always be necessary to send reminders to the targeted users. Dillman (1978) recommends sending up to three reminders over a period of seven weeks.

Data Analysis

Data should be analyzed in a systematic manner. First, the completed forms must be reviewed for errors and missing values. Second, the data must be encoded so that they can be converted into a computerized format. Third, the encoded data must be processed for analysis. Statistical, database, and spreadsheet software packages exist that will perform this function (Van House, 1990).

The Importance of Longitudinal Data

Although the survey can provide valuable baseline data after the initial distribution, the real value of the instrument comes with repeatedly surveying the user community. Repeated surveying and longitudinal analysis will allow administrators to track their progress in improving services and correcting problems. It will also identify changes in the expectations and behaviors of the user community.

Customizing the Survey

The user survey offered on the following pages is a *menu* of possible questions and topics for data collection. Users of this manual will want to select topics and questions from the survey to obtain information of particular interest, or obtain that information from specific target groups. In addition, it may be necessary to customize the wording of specific questions to match terminology or phrases in use at a particular campus. *Do not administer this survey without reducing its overall length and customizing it for your particular campus.*

SAMPLE USER SURVEY

In order to assess the performance of this institution's networked computing services, we would like to ask you some questions about how you use the campus computer network. Your responses will help us improve networked computing services. The information that you provide here will be kept confidential.

Thank you for letting us know what you think!

Please put a check mark in the appropriate box. Select only one answer for each question unless stated otherwise.

I. BACKGROUND

A. Who Are You?

1. Are you? ❑ male   ❑ female

2. What is your age? _____

3. Which of the following items <u>best</u> describes your affiliation with the institution?

   ❑ Undergraduate student .... I live ❑ on campus, ❑ off campus
   ❑ Graduate student .... I live ❑ on campus, ❑ off campus
   ❑ Staff
   ❑ Faculty .... ❑ full professor, ❑ assistant professor,
                                                           ❑ associate professor, ❑ instructor
   ❑ Other (specify) _____

4. Which category <u>best</u> describes your situation?

   ❑ Full-time, locally-based student/faculty/staff
   ❑ Part-time, locally-based student/faculty/staff
   ❑ Distance education student/faculty/staff (Learn/teach/work at a location remote from campus.)

5. What is your academic affiliation for your current studies, teaching, or employment?

   ❑ Architecture   ❑ Art
   ❑ Communications/Journalism   ❑ Computer/Information Science
   ❑ Education   ❑ Engineering
   ❑ Information Studies/Library Science   ❑ Law
   ❑ Liberal Arts   ❑ Management/Business Adminstration
   ❑ Medicine   ❑ Music
   ❑ Nursing   ❑ Political Science/International Affairs
   ❑ Physical Science (Biology, Chemistry, etc.)   ❑ Theater (Drama, Dance)
   ❑ Other (specify) _____

6. If you are a student, what is your GPA (Grade Point Average)? If you are not a student, select "not applicable."

❑ Not applicable; I am not a student. ❑ 2.6-3.0

❑ less than 2.0 ❑ 3.1-3.5

❑ 2.0-2.5 ❑ 3.6-4.0

B. Computers

7. Do you have access to a personal computer (not including those in campus computing facilities)?

❑ Yes (Go to question 8.)

❑ No (Please skip question 8. Go directly to question 9.)

> <u>If yes:</u>
>
> 8. Where is this computer located? (Please select all that apply.)
>
> ❑ Residence
>
> ❑ Office
>
> ❑ No specific place; I have a portable computer.

9. How would you rate your computer skills?

❑ Excellent ❑ Fair

❑ Very Good ❑ Poor

❑ Good ❑ I don't know

10. With what type of computer do you have the greatest familiarity?

❑ Macintosh

❑ Windows-based (IBM compatible)

❑ DOS-based (IBM compatible)

❑ Unix-based

❑ Other (specify)_____

❑ Not familiar with any type of computer

11. Was your decision to study, teach, or work at this institution based, in part, on its campus computer network?

❑ Entirely

❑ Very much

❑ Somewhat

❑ A little

❑ Not at all

II. CAMPUS COMPUTER NETWORK

12. Do you connect to the campus computer network from your residence, office, computer cluster, or while traveling? (This means using email, using a public access computer cluster, exploring the internet, etc. by accessing the university's computer system.)

❑ Yes (Go to question 13.)

❑ No (Please skip all the other questions. You have now completed this survey.)

<u>If yes:</u>

13. How often, on average, do you connect to the campus network?

❑ Several times a day   ❑ Every other week
❑ Daily   ❑ Once a month
❑ Several times a week, but not daily   ❑ Less than once a month
❑ Once a week

14. How long, on average, do you stay connected to the campus network per session?

❑ 10 hours or more   ❑ 30 minutes
❑ 5-9 hours   ❑ 15 minutes
❑ 2-4 hours   ❑ 5 minutes
❑ 1 hour   ❑ less than 5 minutes

A. Access from Off-Campus

15. Do you connect to the campus network from off-campus?

❑ Yes (Go to question 16.)

❑ No (Please skip questions 16 through 21. Go directly to question 22.)

<u>If yes:</u>

16. How often, on average, do you connect to the campus network from off-campus?

❑ Several times a day   ❑ Every other week
❑ Daily   ❑ Once a month
❑ Several times a week, but not daily   ❑ Less than once a month
❑ Once a week

17. When do you usually connect to the campus network from off-campus?

❑ Weekdays   ❑ Both
❑ Weekends

18. What time of day do you usually try to connect to the campus network from off-campus? (Please select all that apply.)

❑ 6 AM - 9 AM   ❑ 6 PM - 9 PM
❑ 9 AM - 12 PM   ❑ 9 PM - 12 AM
❑ 12 PM - 3 PM   ❑ 12 AM - 3 AM
❑ 3 PM - 6 PM   ❑ 3 AM - 6 AM

19. To what degree are you satisfied with the availability of dial-in connections when you are trying to connect to the network from off-campus?

❑ Very satisfied   ❑ Unsatisfied
❑ Satisfied   ❑ I don't know
❑ Somewhat unsatisfied

20. How would you rate network reliability when you connect from off-campus? (stalling, crashing, noise, garbled characters, etc.)

❑ Very good   ❑ Somewhat unsatisfactory
❑ Good   ❑ Unsatisfactory
❑ Adequate   ❑ I don't know

21. In general, how would you rate campus computer network security in terms of privacy?

❑ Very good   ❑ Somewhat unsatisfactory
❑ Good   ❑ Unsatisfactory
❑ Adequate   ❑ I don't know

B. Email

22. Do you have an email account through this institution?

❑ Yes (Go to question 23.)
❑ No (Please skip questions 23 through 24. Go directly to question 25.)

   If yes:

   23. Do you use your email account?

   ❑ Yes (Go to question 24.)
   ❑ No (Please skip questions 24 through 28. Go directly to question 29.)

If yes:

24. How often, on average, do you use email?

❑ Several times a day   ❑ Every other week
❑ Daily   ❑ Once a month
❑ Several times a week   ❑ Less than once a month
❑ Once a week

25. How would you rate the *usefulness* of <u>email</u> for each of the following
    activities? (Check the appropriate box.)

1. Very Useful   5. Useless
2. Useful   6. Don't Know
3. Neither Useful nor Useless   7. Never Used it for this Activity
4. Somewhat Useless   8. Not Applicable (I don't do this activity)

	1.	2.	3.	4.	5.	6.	7.	8.
a. Teaching								
b. Research								
c. Class-related communication								
d. Job-related communication								
e. Professional development								
f. Personal use								
g. Entertainment								

26. Are you subscribed to any listservs (electronic mailing/distribution lists)
    or do you read newsgroup messages?

❑ Yes (Go to question 27.)
❑ No (Please skip questions 27 and 28. Go directly to question 29.)

If yes:

27. How many listservs are you subscribed to or newsgroups do you
    regularly read?

❑ 1-5   ❑ 6-10   ❑ 11-15   ❑ more than 15

28. How would you rate the *usefulness* of <u>listservs and/or newsgroups</u> for each
of the following activities? (Check the appropriate box.)

1. Very Useful
2. Useful
3. Neither Useful nor Useless
4. Somewhat Useless

5. Useless
6. Don't Know
7. Never Used It
8. Not Applicable (I don't do this activity)

	1.	2.	3.	4.	5.	6.	7.	8.
a. Teaching								
b. Research								
c. Class-related communication								
d. Job-related communication								
e. Professional development								
f. Personal use								
g. Entertainment								

C. Other Internet Use

29. Do you use the campus network for internet applications (telnet, gopher, FTP, WWW, IRC, etc.) other than emal or newsgroups?

❑ Yes (Go to question 30.)
❑ No (Please skip questions 30 through 31. Go directly to question 32.)

<u>If yes:</u>

30. How often, on average, do you use the campus network for <u>internet applications</u> other than email? (Check the appropriate box.)

1. Several times a day
2. Daily
3. Several times a week
4. Once a week

5. Every other week
6. Once a month
7. Less than once a month
8. Never used it

	1.	2.	3.	4.	5.	6.	7.	8.
a. Telnet								
b. Gopher								
c. File transfer protocol (FTP)								
d. World wide web (WWW)								
e. Internet Relay Chat (IRC)								
f. Other (specify) _____								

31. How would you rate the *usefulness* of the following <u>internet applications</u> for each of the following activities?

<u>Circle the number which best describes your rating:</u>

1. Very Useful
2. Useful
3. Somewhat Useless

4. Useless
5. Don't Know/Never Used It
6. Not Applicable (I don't do this activity)

	Telnet	Gopher	FTP	WWW	IRC	Other
a. Teaching	1 2 3 4 5 6	1 2 3 4 5 6	1 2 3 4 5 6	1 2 3 4 5 6	1 2 3 4 5 6	1 2 3 4 5 6
b. Research	1 2 3 4 5 6	1 2 3 4 5 6	1 2 3 4 5 6	1 2 3 4 5 6	1 2 3 4 5 6	1 2 3 4 5 6
c. Class assignments	1 2 3 4 5 6	1 2 3 4 5 6	1 2 3 4 5 6	1 2 3 4 5 6	1 2 3 4 5 6	1 2 3 4 5 6
d. Job-related activities	1 2 3 4 5 6	1 2 3 4 5 6	1 2 3 4 5 6	1 2 3 4 5 6	1 2 3 4 5 6	1 2 3 4 5 6
e. Professional development	1 2 3 4 5 6	1 2 3 4 5 6	1 2 3 4 5 6	1 2 3 4 5 6	1 2 3 4 5 6	1 2 3 4 5 6
f. Personal use	1 2 3 4 5 6	1 2 3 4 5 6	1 2 3 4 5 6	1 2 3 4 5 6	1 2 3 4 5 6	1 2 3 4 5 6
g. Entertainment	1 2 3 4 5 6	1 2 3 4 5 6	1 2 3 4 5 6	1 2 3 4 5 6	1 2 3 4 5 6	1 2 3 4 5 6

D. Online Library Catalog and Online Library Services

32. Do you access the online library catalog or other online library services from outside the library using the campus network?

❑ Yes (Go to question 33.)

❑ No (Please skip questions 33 and 34. Go directly to question 35.)

<u>If yes:</u>

33. How often, on average, do you access the online library catalog or other online library services from outside of the library using the campus network?

❑ Several times a day
❑ Daily
❑ Several times a week
❑ Once a week

❑ Every other week
❑ Once a month
❑ Less than once a month

34. How would you rate the *usefulness* of <u>having access to the online library catalog and other online library services from outside the library</u> for each of the following activities? (Check the appropriate box.)

    1. Very Useful   5. Useless
    2. Useful   6. Don't Know
    3. Neither Useful nor Useless   7. Never Used It
    4. Somewhat Useless   8. Not Applicable (I don't do this activity)

	1.	2.	3.	4.	5.	6.	7.	8.
a. Teaching								
b. Research								
c. Class assignments								
d. Job-related activities								
e. Professional development								
f. Personal use								
g. Entertainment								

E. Campus Wide Information System

35. Do you use the Campus Wide Information System (CWIS) via the campus network? (A CWIS is a site, usually accessible via gopher or World Wide Web, where you can find information related to the university and student life.)

❑ Yes (Go to question 36.)

❑ No (Please skip questions 36 through 37. Go directly to question 38.)

<u>If yes:</u>

36. How often, on average, do you use the CWIS?

      ❑ Several times a day
      ❑ Daily
      ❑ Several times a week
      ❑ Once a week
      ❑ Every other week
      ❑ Once a month
      ❑ Less than once a month

37. How would you rate the *usefulness* of the <u>CWIS</u> for each of the following
activities? (Check the appropriate box.)

1. Very Useful
2. Useful
3. Neither Useful nor Useless
4. Somewhat Useless

5. Useless
6. Don't Know
7. Never Used It
8. Not Applicable (I don't do this activity)

	1.	2.	3.	4.	5.	6.	7.	8.
a. Teaching								
b. Research								
c. Class-related information								
d. Job-related information								
e. Professional development								
f. Personal use								
g. Entertainment								

F. Institutional/Administrative Data

38. Do you access institutional/administrative data via the campus network? (Checking your
grades or financial aid, processing payroll, ordering supplies, etc.)

❑ Yes (Go to question 39.)
❑ No (Please skip questions 39 and 40. Go directly to question 41.)

<u>If yes:</u>

39. How often, on average, do you access institutional/administrative data via
the campus network?

❑ Several times a day
❑ Daily
❑ Several times a week
❑ Once a week
❑ Every other week
❑ Once a month
❑ Less than once a month

40. How would you rate the *usefulness* of accessing <u>institutional/administrative</u> data for each of the following activities? (Check the appropriate box.)

1. Very Useful	5. Useless	
2. Useful	6. Don't Know	
3. Neither Useful nor Useless	7. Never Used It	
4. Somewhat Useless	8. Not Applicable (I don't do this activity)	

	1.	2.	3.	4.	5.	6.	7.	8.
a. Teaching								
b. Class-related activities								
c. Job-related activities								
d. Personal use								

III. NETWORK SUPPORT

Help services for network-related problems, such as questions about using applications or dialing in from home, are often available from a centralized office or department. The following section refers to those services.

41. Beside each of the questions presented below please indicate (check the appropriate box) whether you were:

1. Extremely satisfied   3. Indifferent   5. Extremely dissatisfied   7. Never used it
2. Satisfied   4. Dissatisfied   6. Don't know

	1.	2.	3.	4.	5.	6.	7.
Email a. To what degree are you satisfied with the *response time* when requesting help through <u>email</u>?							
b. To what degree are you satisfied with the *quality* of the <u>email</u> help service?							
c. To what degree are you satisfied with the *courtesy* of the person(s) who assisted you through <u>email</u>?							
Phone d. To what degree are you satisfied with the *response time* when requesting help over the <u>phone</u>?							
e. To what degree are you satisfied with the *quality* of the <u>phone</u> help service?							
f. To what degree are you satisfied with the *courtesy* of the person(s) who assisted you over the <u>phone</u>?							
Walk-in g. To what degree are you satisfied with the *response time* when requesting <u>walk-in</u> help?							
h. To what degree are you satisfied with the *quality* of the <u>walk-in</u> help service?							
i. To what degree are you satisfied with the *courtesy* of the person(s) who assist you when requesting <u>walk-in</u> help?							

1. Extremely satisfied   3. Indifferent   5. Extremely dissatisfied   7. Never used it
2. Satisfied   4. Dissatisfied   6. Don't know

	1.	2.	3.	4.	5.	6.	7.
Written Help Guides i. To what degree are you satisfied with the *quantity* of topics for which <u>written help guides</u> that are provided?							
j. To what degree are you satisfied with the *quality* of <u>written help guides</u> that are provided?							
Workshops k. To what degree are you satisfied with the *quantity* of <u>workshops</u> that are provided							
l. To what degree are you satisfied with the *quality* of <u>workshops</u> that are provided?							
Overall Quality m. To what degree are you satisfied with the *overall quality* of the help service you receive when you have a network-related problem?							

IV. PUBLIC COMPUTING FACILITIES

Public access computing facilities, such as computer clusters, are provided for students, faculty, and staff and consist of rooms with computers for the campus community to use for word processing, email, internet access, etc. If you have never used public computing facilities, skip questions 42 to 47. Go directly to question 48.

42. Do you ever use a computer cluster on campus?

❑ Yes (Go to question 43.)
❑ No (Please skip question 43 through 47. Go directly to question 48.)

<u>If yes:</u>

43. How often, on average, do you use public computing facilities?

❑ Several times a day
❑ Daily
❑ Several times a week
❑ Once a week
❑ Every other week
❑ Once a month
❑ Less than once a month

44. When do you usually use public computing facilities?

❑ Weekdays
❑ Weekends
❑ Both

45. What time of day do you usually use public computing facilities? (Please select all that apply.)

❑ 6 AM - 9 AM
❑ 9 AM - 12 PM
❑ 12 PM - 3 PM
❑ 3 PM - 6 PM

❑ 6 PM - 9 PM
❑ 9 PM - 12 AM
❑ 12 AM - 3 AM
❑ 3 AM - 6 AM

46. What do you use the public computing facilities for and how often? (Check the appropriate box.)

1. Several times a day
2. Daily
3. Several times a week
4. Once a week

5. Every other week
6. Once a month
7. Less than once a month
8. Never used it

	1.	2.	3.	4.	5.	6.	7.	8.
a. Word processing								
b. Email								
c. Other internet applications (telnet, newsgroups, gopher, etc.)								
d. Spreadsheets								
e. Presentations								
f. Statistics								
g. Simulation								
h. CAD								
i. Programming								
j. Printing								
k. Other (specify): _____								

47. To what degree are you satisfied with the help services available in the public computing facilities?

❏ Extremely satisfied
❏ Satisfied
❏ Indifferent
❏ Dissatisfied

❏ Extremely dissatisfied
❏ Don't Know
❏ Never used it

48. Beside each of the statements presented below please indicate (check the appropriate box) whether you were:

1. Extremely satisfied   3. Indifferent   5. Extremely dissatisfied   7. Never used it
2. Satisfied   4. Dissatisfied   6. Don't know

	1.	2.	3.	4.	5.	6.	7.
a. To what degree are you satisfied with the applications that are being offered in the facilities?							
b. To what degree are you satisfied with computer availability? (Can you get one when you need one?)							
c. To what degree are you satisfied with the kinds of computers that are offered in public computing facilities?							
d. To what degree are you satisfied with the maintenance of the machines?							
e. To what degree are you satisfied with the printers and the printing of documents?							
f. To what degree are you satisfied with the ergonomics of the public computing facilities? (furniture height, design, etc.)							
g. To what degree are you satisfied with the conditions of the room? (lighting, temperature, noise level, cleanliness, etc.)							
h. Overall, to what degree are you satisfied with public computing facilities?							

V. WHAT DO YOU THINK?

49. How would you rate the *overall quality* of the campus network?

❑ Very good   ❑ Somewhat unsatisfactory

❑ Good   ❑ Unsatisfactory

❑ Adequate   ❑ I don't know

50. Would you be willing to pay extra for access to the campus computer network? If so, how much is the most you would be willing to pay?

❑ No, I wouldn't pay for it.   ❑ Yes, I would pay $50-74 per year.

❑ Yes, I would pay less than $25 per year.   ❑ Yes, I would pay $75-99 per year.

❑ Yes, I would pay $25-49 per year.   ❑ Yes, I would pay $100 or more per year.

51. What are some of the <u>best aspects</u> of the campus computer network? (If you need more space than is provided below, please add additional pages.)

A. _____

B. _____

C. _____

D. _____

52. What are some of the <u>improvements</u> that should be made to the campus computer network? (If you need more space than is provided below, please add additional pages.)

A. _____

B. _____

C. _____

D. _____

53. Has having access to the campus computer network changed your academic, business, or social activities? If yes, how? (If you need more space than is provided below, please add additional pages.)

_____

_____

_____

Thanks for your help. Please return this questionnaire to: [add appropriate instructions]

PART V:

THE NEED FOR ASSESSMENT TECHNIQUES

The numerous initiatives associated with developing the National Information Infrastructure in the USA (e.g., National Information Infrastructure Advisory Council, 1995) and throughout the world with the evolving Global Information Infrastructure, have thrust electronic networked computing into a new arena and into new teaching, learning, and research environments. The uses and applications of networking and the Internet continue to grow rapidly while roles and responsibilities of key stakeholders in the networked environment become increasingly blurred. The range of policy issues grows (e.g., acceptable use, intellectual property rights, and equitable access) while questions regarding the effectiveness, efficiency, and impact of the network in academic institutions continue to be poorly defined or monitored (Heterick, 1994).

Proponents for enhancing the academic networked environment may seem to suffer from "technophoria" as to the likely benefits and results of this enhanced networking environment. But the reality is that evidence to support such assertions is either non-existent or anecdotal. In times of budget cuts and institutional retrenchment, faculty, librarians, administrators, and academic computing service providers find it increasingly difficult to justify expenses for purchasing network technology, supporting network services, developing training, or demonstrating that such networks really have an impact on the educational imperatives of the institution or on its longterm strategic goals.

Based on a number of research projects on the development of networked services and digital libraries in academic settings, Covi and Kling (1995, p. 5) conclude:

> Our early observations suggest that universities appear to be steadily drifting into more intensive digital investments with little managerial oversight about the extent to which their investments are effective or efficient, adequate or frugal.

Given the size and extent of such investments, and the wide-spread financial difficulties many institutions of higher education are experiencing, such a conclusion is most troubling.

Until there is a better conceptual framework describing the "academic networked environment" and assessment techniques to describe interactions and services within this environment, campus officials will only guess at what seems to work well and why. They will only be able to guess at which strategies have had the greatest impact for example, on learning; and they will only be able to guess at how best to design better networked services for the future.

Current trends in higher education suggest increased pressures on campus decision makers to reduce or control costs and improve the overall quality of education. Within this context, decision makers will increasingly ask others on campus for *evidence* that particular services and activities contribute to the overall success of the institution, that the networks are operated efficiently, and that they support specific institutional goals. The academic network certainly will be one of those areas that will be scrutinized in such a manner.

Making wise decisions about the planning and future configuration of information technology on campus will likely consume more, rather than less, time in the future. Hahn offers a number of guidelines that can be used in judging proposals for investing in campus technologies (1995). To implement his common sense suggestions, campus officials will need some evidence of costs, use patterns, and an understanding of *users'* views of these new technologies. The commonly heard phrase of "if you build it they will come," may not apply in academic network planning. In the existing context of *finite* or declining resources for networking, the reality oftentimes is that support for a particular service or application means no support for purchase of another application.

Throughout this project, some reviewers told study team members that the networked information infrastructure was a "given." Such a network was essential for the operation of the institution and required little justification. Senior institutional officials and network managers, however, while noting that the network was a "given" also noted that there was virtually no regularly collected and analyzed descriptive information available on their campus as to the uses, users, and costs of the network — nor was there information on the degree to which the campus network contributed to institutional goals. One senior institutional official referred to planning in such an environment as a "nightmare."

Although the network is a "given" in the sense that it has become an essential component of higher education, how it has become essential, how it is used, and with what benefits are less known. Indeed, this manual is the first comprehensive attempt to provide campus officials with options and strategies for assessing the academic networked environment. It is a first attempt to develop reliable information for decision makers to use in planning their networked environment.

As a first attempt in providing options and strategies for assessing the academic networked environment, the authors are well aware of the many additional issues, topics, and problems which could have been addressed or detailed in this manual. Additional discussion as to issues, procedures, examples, and analysis could be included in almost any section of the manual. To some extent, the production of such a manual is a life-long enterprise given the rapidly changing context of networking technologies and the landscape of higher education.

Nonetheless, it is essential that such a manual be developed and made available to the higher education community. The higher education community must begin the process of assessing the academic network and determining the degree to which it is successful and unsuccessful, the degree to which it contributes to accomplishing institutional goals, and the degree to which the network promotes effective learning and teaching. Planning for the future development of campus-wide networking cannot proceed successfully without such knowledge.

It is within this context of learning and experimenting that this manual is made available. As such, it might best be seen as a "beta version" ready for testing, refinement, and re-writing. After its use and implementation at a number of institutions of higher education, the manual can be revised, expanded, and refined to better address the issues and complexities related to assessing the academic networked environment. But this process must begin, and the manual offers a point for this beginning to occur.

Initially, the authors of the manual expected to provide more options and strategies for assessing the impacts from the academic networked environment. But before such impact assessment could occur, there was first a need to simply be able to conduct descriptive assessments of activities and uses of the network. But "simply" being able to conduct such assessments became increasingly complex. Thus, there is still much work to be done in developing options and strategies to conduct descriptive assessments of the networked environment.

The goal, however, of developing sharper tools for assessing impacts must remain as a top priority for evaluation researchers working in this area. Although a number of our existing instruments are still a bit blunt, such assessment instruments are being developed and tested. Only as our tools are tested, refined, and further developed can the higher education community better understand the uses of the academic networked environment and plan for better networks in the future.

APPENDIX A

SELF-ASSESSMENT TOOLS*

* Reprinted with permisison of CAUSE and
  HEIRAlliance, 4840 Pearl East Circle, Suite 302E,
  Bolder, Colorado, 80301 <info@cause.colorado.edu>.

**the association for
managing and using
information technology
in higher education**

Self-Assessment for Campus Information Technology Services

by Linda H. Fleit

Self-Assessment for
Campus Information Technology Services
by Linda H. Fleit

Table of Contents

Published by

CAUSE

**the association for managing and using
information technology in higher education**

Professional Paper Series, #12

About the Author

Linda Fleit *is President of EDUTECH International, a company that specializes in providing colleges and universities with information technology management consulting, technical services, and publications. Prior to founding EDUTECH International, she held IT management positions at Tufts University, Boston College, the Harvard Business School, and the University of Hartford. Fleit is the editor of a monthly newsletter called* The EDUTECH Report. *She is a frequent speaker at IT conferences and author of several CAUSE/EFFECT articles, including one for which she was selected the 1987 CAUSE/EFFECT Contributor of the Year. She has a bachelor's degree in mathematics from Syracuse University and a master's degree in counseling from Tufts University.*

1 INTRODUCTION

If the modern organizational self-improvement quest had a single beginning, it was probably with the publication of *In Search of Excellence* by Thomas Peters and Robert Waterman. Many, many books since then (*A Passion for Excellence* by Peters and Nancy Austin, *The Change Masters* by Rosabeth Moss Kanter, and *High Output Management* by Andrew Grove, just to note a few, not to mention all the more-recent attention on the pursuit of "total quality") have led to an unprecedented amount of scrutiny of—and improvement in—service areas throughout our economy.

Each approach differs slightly from the one just before it; each one has its own strategies, theories, and rationale. But there are three important ideas that consistently thread through these approaches:

- high quality service is desirable

- high quality service is necessary

- high quality service comes from just a very few things

Furthermore, fundamental to each of these ideas is the assumption that *service quality can be measured.* In fact, it turns out that in order to create and maintain the very highest levels of quality, measuring and assessing quality must be done on a regular basis. Excellence should not just be assumed or taken for granted; quality levels need to be explicit, assessed, and publicly communicated.

In practical terms, however, most of us take on such a task only when we think there might be some serious problems in our area, or in order to justify additional funding. Understandable, because measuring and as-sessing quality is not easy to do. Many of the ordinary measures available to typical service organizations, such as repeat customers and strong profitability, are not appropriate in a campus setting where most information technology departments play to a captive audience of users who have no choice but to use their services if they want any services at all. In addition, most campus computer centers have no measures of either profitability or even cost recovery. The number of steady users and the computer center's budget can be identical in two similarly sized computer centers, one delivering high quality services and the other a dismal failure.

Even monitoring the number of user complaints or keeping a problem log is not the answer to the measurement of quality. A department having a larger number of complaints than one on another campus may not necessarily be delivering lower quality services; in fact, the way the complaints are handled is much more indicative of relative service levels. It has been shown over and over that handling a user's complaint or problem in the right way may be the very best method for winning a loyal fan. Similarly, few complaints or a short problem log do not necessarily mean the computer center is doing an excellent job; it may mean the users have become so frustrated by a lack of responsiveness that they have given up complaining.

So it's not a particularly straightforward task to assess quality; certainly results won't come as easily as when we measure CPU cycles or lines of code written in a day. But we have to do it. It's imperative. Why? *Because everyone else on campus already knows the answer.*

2 THIS IS THE RIGHT TIME

While a good argument can be made that assessing quality is an activity that can and should be done anytime, there are two important trends in higher education right now that make this the ideal time to do a self-assessment.

- **Technology today is much more visible—to everyone on campus—than ever before in its history.**

We all remember the days when the only places we found campus computer centers were in the basements of buildings designed and dedicated to other purposes. The computer center was the largely unseen setting of some mysterious activities that occasionally resulted in printed payroll checks, class rosters, and, with some luck, an SPSS printout.

Echoing the depth of its typical physical location, computing has traditionally been very much a bottom-up affair. The areas in which we made our first real impact and progress were in the college's daily, operational activities such as the business office and the registrar's office. Administrative offices that take care of the day-to-day business of the college, the library, and faculty engaged in writing, research, and administratively oriented classroom activities (such as grading and other record-keeping) were all increasingly well served by computing in the late 1980s. We then slowly began to make our way up the managerial ladders into deans' and vice presidents' offices and out to the students themselves, both in their classrooms and in providing them with administrative services.

Today, technology is everywhere (actually, we're getting to the point at which it is *so* everywhere that it's almost invisible again). It is making more and more of an impact on campus, and reaching higher and higher places. As we progress through the 1990s, we are beginning to see more longer-range computerized de-

cision support, more actual hands-on use of microcomputers by higher-level administrators and deans, more use of devices such as electronic mail and conferencing, and more interest by presidents and vice presidents in new technology tools for the future. We are even seeing the work itself begin to change: as technology increasingly penetrates the upper reaches of the campus, new ways of accomplishing old tasks are also beginning to emerge, and we are seeing increasing interest in ideas such as "reengineering."

What does this mean for campus computing? For one thing, it means increased visibility for the service departments themselves. Computer and information technology services is emerging from being a backroom support organization in a basement somewhere and increasingly taking its rightful place as a strategic campus contributor. This is good, of course, and something we all wished for, but it has come at the cost of a lot more scrutiny than we ever had to deal with before. More people noticing what benefits computing brings to the institution means more people paying attention to how much it costs, how many people work in the computer center, how fast the maintenance budget goes up, and how often someone needs to have a desktop machine replaced.

With all of the benefits that have accrued from increased visibility has come the added burden of attention from a lot of worried people. That brings us to the other major trend in higher education today:

- **Colleges and universities are experiencing an almost desperate need for accountability.**

Higher education is increasingly being held accountable by the public. Where are all of the dollars going? Are tuition money, grant and foundation dollars, and government funding being sensibly spent? How well are college students really being educated? Is college today still "worth" attending, and if so, at what price? What is the real purpose of a college education in today's society? These and other soul-searching questions are being asked from virtually all quarters today, including federal and state governments; as a result, higher education is in something of a turmoil in developing and articulating appropriate, well-thought-out, and relevant answers.

The questioning is every bit as intense, and growing increasingly so, internally on campus. How are professors evaluated? Should there be tenure? What should constitute a "core" curriculum? How are top administrators selected? Are we doing enough of the right things for minority and disabled students? Along with these questions, of course, are others concerning resources, and the manner in which they are being spent. Tuition-dependent institutions continue to be concerned about declining enrollments for the 1990s.

Under these circumstances, and especially with computing still being perceived as so expensive, it is quite understandable that hard questions of technological accountability are being asked with increasing frequency. After all, many reason, it makes more sense to have to take a couple of big hits in selected areas than to do an across-the-institution budget reduction. Where do we hit? How about the department we still don't understand very well? The department from which we still have a lot of trouble seeing the return on investment? You know the one— the department mentioned in that article in *The Chronicle of Higher Education*, "The computer center has replaced the library as academe's bottomless pit."[1]

In this climate of accountability, information technology services is at a disadvantage. It has to compete with campus priorities whose benefits may be more immediate or more obvious. Even though there are only a few (usually) who would question whether the computer people are busy (the computer service department is usually an obvious hub of activity), more people than we might realize do question the *value* of what's going on, and whether the campus could be making better choices than continuing to pour money into computers, given limited resources.

There is unquestionably more progress being made in campus technology pursuits, but there is also more of a demand for payoff. More than ever before, benefits

need to be clearly stated, and not just technological benefits for their own sake. New initiatives in computing need to be accompanied by benefits for the campus mission itself; contributions to the furthering of the institution's goals, both academic and administrative, have to be clearly and forcefully expressed.

The combination of greater scrutiny brought on by both increased visibility and a growing demand for accountability make this an excellent time to do an assessment of the institution's information technology.

But why should it be a *self*-assessment?

Those of us who are or have been computing directors may know what it's like to be told by the person we report to that he or she has called in an outside consultant to review our department. If you don't know this experience, you're lucky, since it is probably one of the most painful things one can go through. Your main task becomes trying to maintain an objective, non-defensive, "good-soldier" posture while at the same time trying to defend every decision you've ever made to a group of outsiders who don't have a clue about your real circumstances. The worst part is knowing that the review is being conducted because there is a perception, whether based in reality or not, that your department has some very serious problems it can't take care of itself. The experience is nothing short of excruciating.

And what about outsourcing? In a sense, looking at outsourcing as a way of providing the institution's computing services is another way of asking, "How much are you willing to pay for a high-quality computing environment?" John Gehl, last year in *EDUCOM Review*, reflected on this issue of the relationship between *value* and *evaluation*:

> There used to be a lot of TV ads in which the salesman would add product after product to some fabulous offer of juicers and food processors and utensils and ginzu knives, and after each product was added, the frenzied pitchman would ask the question: "*Now* how much would you pay?" Now *that's* evaluation. It's done all the time in the marketplace. It's deciding what something is worth. In the vernacular, it's putting your money where your mouth is. ... The question at evaluation time isn't whether the ginzu knife was able to dice a carrot or whether the software product had functionality; the question at evaluation time is: Look-

4/ SELF-ASSESSMENT FOR CAMPUS INFORMATION TECHNOLOGY SERVICES

ing back on it from where you are now, what should you have told the fellow when he asked you, *"Now how much would you pay?"*[2]

Outsourcing is not just an alternative to be considered only when the internal people are in trouble; it's being looked at more and more today as a sound financial move—a cost-effective vehicle for providing campus computing services. How many computer directors are surprised when the subject comes up? How many have surprise turn to astonishment when an outsourcing company is actually called in to do an evaluation? How many are just completely unprepared to present their administrations with another alternative to outsourcing based on their own objective assessments of the institution's information technology area? Outsourcing may or may not be a good thing for the institution to do, but it's a sure bet that the institution will be in a better position to make this decision if they have solid, viable alternatives to look at.

It is far, far better to do an assessment yourself before it ever reaches a crisis point. It is so much easier to unearth difficulties and deal with them before they reach a level of visibility that turns them into big problems. It is so much easier to make a rational case for keeping computing services inside when you have time to prepare the case fully, without the Sword of Damocles in the form of an outsourcing threat hanging over your head.

Note, by the way, that doing a self-assessment does not preclude your asking an outsider to assist, whether that is someone from within the institution, or a colleague from another campus, or even a professional consultant. There could very well be some significant benefit gained in the objectivity that an outsider usually brings to an assignment of this sort. But it is still a self-assessment if the person is doing it on your behalf, with the results delivered just to you.

Why not ask the users?

Ed Koch, the former mayor of New York City, used to make a habit of asking, "How am I doing?" to anyone likely to give him an answer. He asked it often and unhesitatingly, even when he suspected the answer was not going to be to his liking. Although Koch is no longer mayor, and although his popularity waned dramatically toward the end of his final term, he is still known and respected for having asked the question.

Asking the users of computer services how the computer services department is doing can yield some very valuable information. It is an important way of staying in touch with the users, and of preventing the department from becoming too isolated and solely self-appraising. Asking users their opinions may produce some surprises, or it may confirm what is already known; in either case, it is something that should be done regularly, in both formal and informal ways. However, asking the users to participate in this self-assessment is not appropriate. While, for at least part of the assessment, it is going to be very important to try to see things from the users' point of view, their actual views are not relevant to this purpose, and soliciting them will only be distracting.

That may sound strange given the current politically correct emphasis on customer service, but it isn't really. A self-assessment allows an internal focus and an emergence of an inner-directed evaluation. As individuals, it is important to hear what others think of us, but it is also important (and involves a different task) to ask what we think of ourselves and to try to answer as honestly as possible. It is no different for a department. The locus of evaluation in this case is internal; assessments from external sources require a different strategy.[3]

Who should do a self-assessment?

Everyone should do a self-assessment, at least once a year. Even if you think that you're doing the very best job you could possibly do; that you have the best, most dedicated staff; that users are being very well treated and the administration is being very well served; that funding your department is absolutely the wisest way for the institution to spend its technology dollars, you should do a self-assessment. If you are right about your sense of quality, then the assessment will confirm it with an objective process that you can use as a communications vehicle to others. If you are wrong, you'll have an opportunity to correct your problems before they get out of hand.

---

[1] *Chronicle* of *Higher Education*, 2 May 1990, p. A15.

[2] John Gehl, "Nine Cents' Worth," *EDUCOM Review*, March/April 1993, p. 17.

[3] "Asking the Users: How Are We Doing?" *The EDUTECH Report*, May 1991.

3 WHAT A SELF-ASSESSMENT IS

The self-assessment offered here is meant to be used by all higher education institutions. It doesn't matter whether the school is public or private, large or small, rich or poor. It doesn't matter how long the institution has had computing facilities, nor whether they are organized in particular ways. The questions will apply in almost every circumstance, and form a package that accomplishes four important tasks.

- **A self-assessment is preventive medicine.**

First, and most important, a self-assessment is preventive medicine. Just like vitamins or an aerobic exercise regimen, a self-assessment can be an invaluable tool in preventing major problems from happening in the first place. For instance, gaining the realization through a self-assessment that one of the things the information technology department ought to be doing is constructing more formal project plans with a great deal of user participation may very well prevent the next major project from going seriously awry.

A self-assessment is an anticipatory mechanism; it is a way to find the kinds of things that should be modified to enhance the computer center's operations and services, and a way to look for signals that there is trouble brewing. Used in this mode, it is proactive instead of reactive; it is a way to break away from constantly putting out fires by finding ways to promote fire safety and prevention.

- **A self-assessment is a diagnostic tool.**

Second, this assessment is a diagnostic tool for a computer services department in trouble and, further, it can provide a roadmap to improvement. When *The EDUTECH Report* published an article on self-assessment a couple of years ago,[4] one of the most interesting

responses came from a financial vice president, to whom his institution's computer center reported. He thought the methodology and the sample questions the article outlined were interesting, but doubted that most computer center directors would be inclined to do such an assessment, thereby eventually forcing the need to have an evaluation done by outsiders. He went on to say that the only computer center that would do a self-assessment is the one that doesn't need to.

That could be true if the purpose of the assessment was to figure out where to place blame. But that isn't the point at all. The point is to figure out what's wrong, to identify those factors that are contributing to a less-than-highest-quality computing environment, and then to attack those problems. It doesn't really matter how the problems got there, or who made what decision way back when that led to all this; what matters most is the diagnosis and, based on that, the cure. Saying that the only departments who will do this are the ones who don't need to is the same as saying that the only people who will have their blood tested when they feel overly thirsty all the time are the ones who don't have diabetes.

- **A self-assessment is a comparative measure.**

Third, a self-assessment is a way to get a comparative measure—but only against potential. That is, the major question that a self-assessment asks is, "How well are we doing, *relative to how well we could be doing*?" This is not the same question as, "How well are we doing relative to other institutions?" There are no numeric scores here; this tool will not lead to the higher education version of the *Computerworld 100*.[5] Its purpose is to assess how well the information technology service department is doing the job it has been given to do.

6/ SELF-ASSESSMENT FOR CAMPUS INFORMATION TECHNOLOGY SERVICES

It is also not the same question as, "How well are we doing relative to some arbitrary ideal?" Nor is it a trend analysis; it does not ask, "How well are we doing relative to how well we used to do in the past?" The point is to compare the information technology services department to its own potential. The potential is always relative; it depends on the department's level of resources, the place it occupies in the institution's hierarchy, the legacy of hardware and software decisions that were made in the past, and a whole host of other factors.

It doesn't matter if Majoreastcoast University has brought CAD/CAM capability to every dorm room and you haven't; it doesn't matter if every book you read tells you that you should have implemented wireless communications by now and you haven't; and it doesn't matter if you are maintaining 500 microcomputers this year and last year it was only 400. While all of these comparisons have importance in some sense, they are not part of a self-assessment. What really counts here is whether you are doing the right things and doing them well, given what's possible under your particular circumstances.

- **A self-assessment promotes alignment with users' assessments**

Finally, a self-assessment is a way to more closely align one's own evaluation of quality with the receiver's (user's) evaluation, whether the latter is explicit or not. Up to now, if we measured anything, it was only those things relatively easy to measure: lines of code per day, number of CPU cycles, percent of mainframe downtime, numbers of microcomputers. When all of those numbers seem satisfactory, or fall within the "right" ranges, it may be difficult to understand why the users don't seem happy. One of the important things we are beginning to realize now is that these quantitative measures do not get at the heart of the issue, which is whether the information technology department is actually doing a good job, as seen by its customers and by institutional management.

Earlier, you read the answer to the question concerning why a self-assessment is imperative: "Because everyone else on campus already knows the answer." They do. They may not have articulated it yet, but every user on campus, and every person in the administration and among the faculty who is concerned with the way the institution spends its money, already has a percep-

tion of the information technology services on campus. In general, that perception will have less to do with how much (or how little) disk space there is than with how much technical jargon the computer people use when they talk to others. Doing this self-assessment will help you identify why the campus community's perception is the way it is, and, if necessary, how the perception can be improved.

How does a self-assessment differ from an audit?

It is important to keep in mind that a self-assessment is not an audit. The purpose is not to look for areas of control or potential mischief; the emphasis is not on compliance, asset protection, reliability and accuracy of data, or any of those audit-oriented subjects. The questions are designed to examine issues at a more strategic level than in an audit; that is, although they do encourage a deeper look than might be done ordinarily, they are not as detailed or as control-oriented as the ones an auditor would ask. The answers are meant to provide insight into the broad array of services the department offers, and the manner in which those services are administered and delivered.

In addition, the assessment is designed to elicit information, not just data. The answers are meant to be weighed and judged, and are open to a certain amount of interpretation. Many of the answers will be more subjective than objective, and none will be answered numerically.

Most importantly, the focus of a self-assessment is on *effectiveness*, assessing the quality and quantity of technology resources, the department's responsiveness, and the policies that promote effectiveness. The focus of a traditional audit is on *efficiency* and control, the use of resources relative to the production of output, and the procedures used to make things efficient and under control.

---

4 "Be Your Own Consultant: Review Computer Services," *The EDUTECH Report*, April 1989.

5 The *Computerworld 100* is an annual quantitative ranking of the top 100 organizations, measured by the effectiveness of their use of information technology. It is organized by industry, but does not include education, higher or otherwise.

4 THE MECHANICS

There are just four basic steps in a self-assessment: asking the questions, answering them, evaluating the results, and constructing an action plan based on what the results reveal.

The actual doing of a self-assessment should not be so burdensome that people will run shrieking in the hallways at the prospect of it. To give the whole thing credibility, it should be defined as a formal project, with a beginning and an end, and the head of the information technology department being assessed should be the project manager. However, the assessment itself should take no longer than a week or two, perhaps longer in large institutions, with the writing up of the results taking a bit longer. There is not much, if any, research required to answer the questions, since they are much more qualitative than quantitative. These are usually the sorts of issues that people can respond to directly, without having to look things up, so the assessment is not particularly difficult in terms of information gathering.

The assessment can be used for the entire range of information technology services on campus, or only for a piece of it; for instance, it could be used at one time just for computer services, leaving out telecommunications, audio-visual, and so on, and then at another time, it could include everything. If there is more than one computer center being administered by a single department, the assessment should include all of them at once. However, if there are separate departments for administrative and academic computing, the assessment for each should be done independently. (Comparing the results could be very interesting!)

As many internal information technology staff as possible should be involved in thinking about and answering the questions. For large departments, small group meetings are usually the best way to go, although not necessarily organized along division or position lines. That is, it is likely to be more fruitful if the group answering the questions is made up of a mixture of people, including programmers, operators, user support people, and so on, rather than just one type. In a smaller department, one or two meetings of the whole department will probably be all that's necessary to complete the assessment. In all cases, the results should be distributed back to all who participated.

One of the most important things to remember is that because this is being done internally, there is nothing to defend. The point of the assessment is not to fix blame or to rehash the past. The point is to identify areas of improvement for the future. Therefore, it's in everyone's best interests to be as honest as possible. Again, it may help to use an outsider to assist, but that is not a necessity.

About the questions

The questions in the assessment (which are found in Appendix A) are arranged into six categories: planning, policies and procedures, facilities and staff, products and services, organization and external relationships, and funding. The questions have been developed through a combination of many years of talking with higher education information technology managers; many discussions with other higher education people, including presidents, deans, and chief financial officers; and a great deal of reading about what makes an information technology organization effective. Based on those discussions, observations, and experience, the questions were developed to have a direct relationship between the answers and the probable implications and consequences of the answers.

8/ SELF-ASSESSMENT FOR CAMPUS INFORMATION TECHNOLOGY SERVICES

It is possible that as you read through the questions you may see things that may not appear to be relevant or important in assessing your department. For example, you may think it's okay to have service priorities determined internally in the department. That's the way it's always been, and it seems to work most of the time; besides, most of the users, and certainly most or all of the upper administration, do not want to get involved in this. You and your people are smart enough and have been around long enough to determine what's best for the school. So your answer to the question, "Is priority setting controlled by the users and accountable to the administration?" will be "no," and you might also add, "But so what? It's not a problem that we do it this way." But, in fact, it is a problem or, at least, an incipient one. It has been shown time after time, in countless institutions, that as the demand for services grows, deciding who gets which services eventually puts the computer department in a classic no-win situation. You will have to turn down more and more requests, you will face increasing risk of alienating all end users at one time or another, you will continuously have to rely on your own judgement about what's best for the school, and, inevitably, the wrong person is going to get so angry with you and your department that there will be a major crisis. No matter how fast you dance, or how well you juggle, you will never be able to keep up with the demand and keep everyone happy. You don't need to be the bad guy; what you need is to have the users determining among themselves what's best and then looking to you to be the heroic implementor of their decisions.

In a case like this, there is a certain amount you may need to take on faith. Each question was put into the assessment deliberately, and while it would be difficult to make the case that any "no" answer automatically spells trouble, a question that is answered with a "no," "maybe," or anything less than "yes" at least suggests that the topic could probably use further scrutiny. A great many negative answers probably indicates that the department is either already in, or rapidly approaching, big trouble. On a more positive note, if all or even most of the answers are "yes," then it is probably fair to say that the department is in terrific shape. The greater the number of positive answers, the more assurance the computer services department and others on campus have that things are going well and will continue to go well.

Many of the questions will require you to look at situations from the users' point of view, and to presume what their answers might be to the same questions. You may find it more difficult to answer these, but in many cases your presumption of the answer may be as important as the real answer itself. This is especially true if you decide to follow up the self-assessment with a user survey. Testing your presumptions through a user survey will very likely turn out to be an important and interesting thing to do, although, as mentioned above, asking the users their opinions is not a formal part of this self-assessment process.

Not all of the answers are black or white. Some are, but many are meant to be deliberately thought-provoking and not easily answerable off the cuff. Taken as a whole, they add up to a picture of a well-balanced, effective, high-quality information technology service.

5 DEALING WITH THE RESULTS

By its nature, the assessment will reveal interesting results. Some of these may come as a surprise; some may merely confirm what everyone in the department already knew. In either case, the results should lead to a plan of action.

In the happy circumstance of a wholly positive assessment, the results should be shared with others in whatever way is appropriate. Of course, an information technology services department in this situation will already be held in high esteem on campus, but including the assessment in the department's annual report, for instance, would be a good way to communicate the department's high level of quality without being self-aggrandizing.

The harder situation, of course, is when the assessment turns out to be less than positive. In this case, the results need not be shared with others outside the department; in fact, no one else even needs to know the assessment was done. However, it is important to bear in mind that a lot of negative answers probably indicates that problems are showing up externally anyway. Basically, the department has two alternatives for the next step:

- **Alternative 1: Ignore the results and hope this will all go away.**

This will likely be the most tempting alternative, since it involves doing pretty much the same thing as before. It also can easily be justified by focusing on why "the problems aren't my/our fault": we don't have enough money; the users are too demanding; my boss doesn't understand technology; my boss doesn't understand me (us); the users haven't made enough of an investment to make their computing pay off; all of the above.

The risk in pursuing this alternative is obvious: eventually someone is going to demand an accounting, and you will most likely end up on the receiving end of an outside assessment (and maybe worse). No one will care about the reasons given above, especially the outside consultants called in to do the assessment; they have heard it all before (yawn). There is a much better alternative.

- **Alternative 2: Develop an improvement plan.**

Begin with the assumption that a "no" answer to any question may indicate a problem, even if that problem has not yet manifested itself. Then look at the area in which the greatest proportion of negative answers emerged, decide whether the negative answers really are indicative of problems or potential problems in your particular circumstances (try to be as objective as possible about this), decide whether it's something that can be fixed, and fix it. In many cases, the solution won't even cost anything (in dollars, that is).

Too simple? Remember, the questions were designed to evaluate quality and effectiveness; "no" answers reveal gaps in the ingredients for success, *even if the lack of success hasn't shown up yet.* Filling in the gaps now, beginning with the areas of the greatest number of negative answers, will prevent failure from ever showing its ugly head.

Of course, there will be some things beyond your control. For instance, it isn't necessarily up to you to determine the level of funding the institution is prepared to provide for information technology, or whether to have a high-level policy committee. However, it is entirely possible that you have more control than you think. Start with a positive stance. Assume that you can at least have an influence on these things, even if they

10/ SELF-ASSESSMENT FOR CAMPUS INFORMATION TECHNOLOGY SERVICES

are not directly subject to your control. Sometimes that influence can turn out to be major, or you may be able to influence someone who can influence someone else. The point is to not simply shrug off certain areas just because they are outside your direct domain.

It is also important not to be distracted or deterred by red herrings. It is too convenient an excuse for inaction, for instance, to blame limited resources for everything. But a close examination of whatever negative answers have emerged in your assessment may very well show that it isn't a money issue at all; it's an attitude change that's needed, or a new procedure that needs to be developed, or a new approach to service delivery. It may be entirely possible to effect positive changes without spending a cent.

What if the assessment is wrong?

In general, the results of the assessment should match your intuition—if, that is, you are being honest with yourself. If they do not, and you think the assessment may be wrong (that is, you show more negative answers than you think are really indicative of problems), then maybe it is. The questionnaire is not perfect. It may not match your particular circumstances well enough, or you may find you need to adapt it to your institution and your department. But you need to be careful here that you are not falling into the very understandable temptation to close your eyes to the truth. If you are, it is absolutely inevitable that eventually someone will open your eyes for you.

Ideally, the assessment will pinpoint areas that need some attention, areas where you may have been experiencing feelings too vague to deal with ("Something's wrong but I don't know what it is ..." or "I think we're basically doing okay, but maybe we could be doing better ..."). Often just the process of doing the assessment is beneficial in bringing people in the department together and focusing on the right issues. In such a case, whether the results are positive or negative, and whether they are accurate or inaccurate, something has been gained.

Excellent IT services

As Brian Hawkins wrote in the book he edited for the EDUCOM Strategy Series, *Organizing and Managing Information Resources on Campus:*

All of us involved in providing and supporting information resources on our campuses must constantly remind ourselves of the ultimate objective of what we are doing, namely, facilitating the scholarship of students and faculty. Except in a very few disciplines, technology is not an end in and of itself—it is the means to achieve some other scholarly aim. Technology, however, has an allure and a seductiveness that occasionally catches all of us, and we forget the original goal as we become captivated with the process.[6]

What, then, are the true ingredients for excellence? On the whole, two characteristics mark the excellent campus information technology service department, and they both fall directly out of the "ultimate objective" Hawkins talks about. The first is that it assists in the efforts to provide and improve the quality of education. The second is that it assists in lowering the cost of administering and delivering that education. In other words, the information technology services provided by the excellent computer center, by contributing directly to the goals of its institution, help make the institution both more effective and more efficient.

It is incumbent upon us, as higher education information technology professionals, to strive for excellence. The information technology department is one of the few departments on campus whose services are highly visible to so many people, and whose services affect on a day-to-day basis the personal productivity of faculty, students, and administrators. It is also one of the few departments with such a large budget. We just have to be as good as possible. It is, therefore, very important to keep asking ourselves how well we are doing.

> Excellence is a game of inches, or millimeters. No one act is, *per se*, clinching. But a thousand things, a thousand thousand things, each done a tiny bit better, do add up to memorable responsiveness and distinction ... .
>
> Tom Peters and Nancy Waters
> *A Passion For Excellence*

---

[6] Brian L. Hawkins, *Organizing and Managing Information Resources on Campus* (McKinney, Texas: Academic Computing Publications, 1989), p. 11.

Appendix A: Self-Assessment Questions

Section 1: Planning

A. Strategic and long-range planning

☐ Is there a multi-year plan for computing and telecommunications in place for the whole institution?

☐ If so, was it drawn from institutional objectives, even if those objectives are not fully articulated?

☐ Was the planning process a participative and collaborative one?

☐ Is the plan updated on a regular basis, such as once a year?

☐ Is the plan written in non-technical language with goals and objectives that are meaningful to a broad base of campus people?

B. Operational planning

☐ Is there a one-year operational plan in place, with a projected budget?

☐ Are annual reports done to show actual activities and expenditures compared with what was planned?

C. Disaster recovery planning

☐ Is there a written disaster recovery plan in place?

☐ Has it actually been tested?

☐ Does it include office-based systems as well as the computer center?

☐ Does it include academic computing facilities?

☐ Does it include the telecommunications network?

D. Project planning

☐ Are there formal, written project plans for every major project the information technology services department undertakes?

☐ Have the users participated in creating these plans?

☐ Do the plans specify project goals and objectives, deliverables, budgets, responsibilities, staffing levels, and deadlines?

☐ Are the project plans constructed with the understanding that there will be changes to the deliverables and that a change order process is needed?

Section 2: Policies and Procedures

A. Customer service

☐ Is a service orientation promoted and well understood throughout the department?

☐ Are users always well treated and responded to in appropriate ways?

12/ SELF-ASSESSMENT FOR CAMPUS INFORMATION TECHNOLOGY SERVICES

☐ If the users had to pay for the department's services with real money, would they?

B. Service level agreements

☐ Are there written service level agreements between the information technology department and its users?

☐ Do they cover every major service provided by the department?

☐ Have these agreements resulted from a negotiation process involving the users and taking into account current resource levels?

C. Status reports

☐ Are regular status reports issued to the campus community to describe current usage levels, the tasks awaiting action in each of the service queues, and expected time to resolution?

D. Priority setting

☐ Is the priority-setting process for the department objective and well understood?

☐ Is it controlled by the users and accountable to the administration?

☐ Can the process be bypassed for emergency work without creating a crisis?

☐ Is the work backlog short enough not to discourage people from asking for reasonable requests?

☐ Is everyone clear on how new technology initiatives are justified?

E. Standards

☐ Are there hardware, software, and procedural standards that both computer staff and users are encouraged to follow?

☐ Are programs always written the same way, using reusable code and libraries whenever possible?

☐ Are there choices within the standards that allow users to retain some local control?

☐ Does the department staff widely promote ethical computing to the institution?

F. Security

☐ Are the computing facilities secure?

☐ Is data security taken seriously?

☐ Does the security function include procedures for department staff as well as guidelines for users for decentralized data and equipment?

☐ Are there sufficient edits to make sure bad data do not enter any of the systems?

☐ Are there watchdog procedures to make sure unauthorized access to data is recorded and followed up on?

G. Problem tracking

☐ Is there a system in place for recording, tracking, and resolving problems ?

☐ Is it clear to the users whom to call for help?

☐ Is there an emergency user notification process in place for such things as machine outages?

H. Inventories

☐ Are inventories kept of all computing resources, including microcomputers, terminals, printers, and supplies?

Section 3: Facilities and Staff

A. User access

☐ Are facilities in convenient and safe locations?

☐ Are all of the services and facilities provided by the department easy to access, and easy to obtain assistance for?

☐ Are facilities in convenient and safe locations?

☐ Would a new user know where to go to get involved with computing?

☐ Is there user documentation for every service area in the department?

☐ Is it well written and accurate?

B. Utilization reports

☐ Are there formal ways of measuring actual usage of each of the major services areas within the computer department, such as mainframe(s) CPU hours, online transactions, programming hours, printed pages, help desk requests, microcomputer allocations, e-mail messages, etc.?

C. Capacity planning

☐ Are usage statistics checked regularly against capacity on items such as mainframe response time, operator overtime hours, and disk storage?

☐ Are there established ways of dealing with both under- and over-utilization?

D. Productivity tools

☐ Are fourth-generation tools, such as non-procedural programming languages, relational database management systems, and CASE tools, either in use already or planned for near-future use?

☐ Are they, or will they be, accessible by both administrative and academic users?

E. Research and development

☐ Is there a "research and development" function within the department to assure that technical innovations and recent developments are not overlooked?

F. Staff background and experience

☐ Do all staff members have experience in higher education?

☐ Are the "politics" of higher education institutions an accepted part of the work environment?

☐ Do the staff who work directly with end users understand the users' work environments, including goals and objectives?

☐ Do all staff members have enough technical expertise?

☐ Do most or all staff members use microcomputers?

☐ Does everyone in the department have excellent interpersonal communications skills, both orally and in writing?

G. Staff training

☐ Is there a formal staff training and education program?

☐ Is it reviewed on a regular basis to make sure it is up to date and serving genuine staff needs?

☐ Is it geared toward the higher education environment?

☐ Are the skills and talents of the staff well matched with user service needs, as opposed to the department's perception of service needs being shaped by the staff's current strengths and capabilities?

☐ Are staff members cross-trained so that service areas are not vulnerable to someone's absence?

H. Staff attitude

☐ Do staff members see themselves as productive work partners with their users?

☐ Do they have high self-esteem without being arrogant or unapproachable?

☐ Is morale in the department good?

☐ Does the staff feel well rewarded for its efforts?

14/ SELF-ASSESSMENT FOR CAMPUS INFORMATION TECHNOLOGY SERVICES

☐ Is everyone in the department clear on what is expected from them?

I. Staff turnover

☐ Is the turnover rate among the computing staff at a high enough level to regularly bring in fresh ideas, but low enough so that it is not disruptive?

☐ Are open positions filled relatively quickly?

☐ Are compensation strategies (taking into account benefits and intangibles) competitive, or at least reasonable?

J. Student employees

☐ Does the center make use of student workers in every case where feasible?

☐ Are the students encouraged to see themselves as staff members, with corresponding rights and responsibilities, especially concerning data security, reliability of performance, and attitude?

☐ Do students generally tend to stay with the department throughout their academic careers?

Section 4: Products and Services

A. Direction

☐ Are the department's products and services moving toward a distributed computing environment?

☐ Is the department's philosophy supportive of self-sufficiency for end users?

☐ Are there tools available to promote end-user computing, such as a report writer, download software, and a query capability,?

B. Architecture

☐ Is the system architecture sufficiently flexible to promote end-user computing and control?

☐ Is the right combination of mainframes, microcomputers, and minicomputers used to provide solutions to end users?

☐ Are data definitions consistent and understood by all those creating and having access to data?

☐ Is the data communications network widespread throughout campus?

C. Applications development

☐ Are there formal ways of determining which applications should be supported by purchased software, which should be developed in-house, and which should be a combination of the two?

D. Delivery

☐ Are projects always completed on time?

☐ Are deadlines always met?

☐ Are budgets always adhered to?

☐ Are the deliverables always perceived as valuable by the recipients?

☐ Does the department always fulfill its service level commitments?

E. User Training

☐ Is there a training strategy for users?

☐ Does it make the best use of a variety of resources, including self-paced instruction, classroom training, one-on-one assistance, and video?

F. Quality assurance

☐ Is there a formal quality assurance function in the department?

☐ Does it have oversight on all service matters, including program maintenance, administrative production, mainframe response time, data security and integrity, etc.?

G. Backlog

☐ Is the backlog of service requests, especially for applications programming changes and enhancements, at a reasonable level?

☐ Is it short enough so as not to build up a "hidden" demand or guilt on the part of users in asking for something?

H. Outreach

☐ Does the department have a customer outreach function?

☐ Are there ways to let academic and administrative users know about technological innovations in their areas and new sources of materials and information?

☐ Are users regularly canvassed to determine how the department can be helpful to them?

Section 5: Organization and External Relationships

A. Organization

☐ Are the institution's information technology services organized in such a way as to promote both economies of scale and end-user responsiveness?

☐ Has the institution achieved the right balance of centralization and decentralization so that the entire community is being well served in the most cost-efficient ways?

☐ Is there sufficient coordination among related service areas to assure the institution that everyone is moving in the same direction?

B. Reporting

☐ Does the computer services department report to the right level within the institution?

☐ Does it report to a person knowledgeable enough about computing issues to be able to provide substantive guidance and support?

☐ Does the president support information technology for the institution as a whole?

Does the department get enough of the right kind of attention?

C. Advisory committees

☐ Is there a computing advisory committee made up of high-level faculty and administrators to advise on broad policy and priority matters?

☐ Does this group meet at least twice a year?

D. Users groups

☐ Is there a users group (or perhaps more than one) that discusses operational matters and helps resolve priority issues and matters of resource allocations among computing services users?

☐ Does this group meet at least six times a year?

E. Data security and integrity

☐ Are users responsible for the data kept on computers?

☐ Is there a consistent flow of data throughout the institution so that processing cycles, census dates, and backup procedures are both understood and used by everyone?

F. External support

☐ Are there resources on campus, in addition to the computer services department, that are also supporting users' needs?

☐ Are there library staff members, department-based "power users," or application-specific users groups (such as microcomputing) from which users can get help or advice?

16/ Sᴇʟꜰ-Aꜱꜱᴇꜱꜱᴍᴇɴᴛ ꜰᴏʀ Cᴀᴍᴘᴜꜱ Iɴꜰᴏʀᴍᴀᴛɪᴏɴ Tᴇᴄʜɴᴏʟᴏɢʏ Sᴇʀᴠɪᴄᴇꜱ

G. User expectations

☐ Are expectations of end users realistic, given the institution's funding of information technology, capabilities of current technology, and their own perceptions of what their investment needs to be (education and training, participation in planning and setting priorities, providing specifications, review, and evaluation of deliverables)?

H. User satisfaction

☐ Are the users' perceptions about both the quality and quantity of computer services favorable?

☐ If the computer department were in a competitive situation, would it retain its customer base?

☐ Are the users generally willing to abide by the guidelines and standards set by the computing department?

☐ Are user satisfaction surveys conducted on a regular basis?

☐ Do the users hold the department's staff members with whom they work in great esteem?

I. Management satisfaction

☐ Are the administration's perceptions of the efficiency and effectiveness of computer services favorable?

☐ Does the department have influence with decision-makers?

☐ Is the person in charge of information technology services thought of as a part of the institution's "management team"?

☐ Do top-level people make regular use of the department's facilities and services?

J. Communications

☐ Are there both formal (regular meetings, newsletters, open door hours) and informal ways of communicating with others on campus?

☐ Are they used by everyone in the department?

K. Credibility

☐ Does the department have credibility on campus?

☐ Are the staff's opinions sought and valued?

☐ Is the department a regular participant in other planning activities, such as new building construction or building renovation, capital campaign planning, enrollment management, and so forth?

Section 6: Funding

A. Level

☐ Is funding at an appropriate level to support the institution's technology goals?

☐ Does the level of funding accurately reflect the level of importance that technology has to and for the institution?

☐ Does information technology services receive a steady percentage of the institution's budget from year to year?

B. Funding requests

☐ Do requests for funding for additional resources (programming time, microcomputers, disk space, etc.) come from the users, rather than from the computing department?

C. User awareness

☐ Are all users aware of the cost of computing?

☐ Is there a mechanism (for example, a charge-out system) which encourages users to make use of computing services in an efficient manner?

☐ If there is no charge-out, do users have to justify their requests for services in some way to the people to whom they report?

☐ Do users make educated requests by appreciating and understanding fully the costs (dollars, time, etc.) and consequences (adjustment of their and others' deadlines) of their requests?

D. Gifts

☐ Are donations and gifts-in-kind actively solicited from alumni and companies?

☐ Are the activities of the computing department presented in such a way that donors are motivated to give support to these efforts?

☐ Are computing initiatives included in grant proposals and, if there is one, in the capital campaign?

☐ Are there guidelines for the solicitation and acceptance of technology gifts to the institution?

☐ Is there a way of ensuring both consistency and usefulness of any hardware, software, or communications products that might be donated?

E. Capital budgeting

☐ Is there a capital budgeting process for information technology to minimize unexpected costs and to provide for orderly growth?

☐ Is a replacement or depreciation factor built in?

F. Generating income

☐ Have ways to develop income been explored?

☐ Has a student fee or a tuition increase been considered?

☐ Is there a possibility of selling technology resources to outsiders (for instance, microcomputer training)?

☐ Are grant opportunities pursued on a regular basis?

☐ Has the institution thought about reselling telephone services, cable TV services, and/or computers to students?

G. Outsourcing

☐ Has outsourcing some or all of the information technology services been explored?

APPENDIX B

The *CAUSE/EDUCOM Evaluation Guidelines for Institutional Information Technology Resources* are reprinted here with permission from CAUSE and EDUCOM. CAUSE is a nonprofit professional association whose mission is to enhance the administration and delivery of higher education through the effective management and use of information technology in colleges and universities, and to help individual members develop as professionals in the field of information technology management in higher education. EDUCOM is a nonprofit consortium of higher education institutions which facilitates the introduction, use, access to, and management of information resources in teaching, learning, scholarship, and research. Since the publication of these guidelines, CAUSE and EDUCOM have been joined by the Association of Research Libraries in the creation of the Higher Education Information Resources Alliance (HEIRAlliance), which plans to undertake a revision of these guidelines in 1994 to recognize the increasing importance of networking information resources and its impact on academic libraries.

EVALUATION GUIDELINES
FOR INSTITUTIONAL
INFORMATION TECHNOLOGY RESOURCES †

The purpose of this document is to provide institutions and regional accrediting associations with evaluation guidelines for information technology resources that they could use as a reference when developing their own standards for this area. These guidelines have been developed based on accreditation team experiences. They also have been reviewed and endorsed by the CAUSE and EDUCOM Boards, two key organizations in the information technology field in higher education (see back page).

INTRODUCTION

In the last decade, institutions of higher education have invested heavily in information technology resources. In particular, the availability of low cost, high powered desktop workstations has accelerated the move to distributed computing and high speed local and national networks. Organizational structures, often the most traditional parts of our universities, have been changing in response to the growing importance of information technology resources to the achievement of institutional missions.

Recently, calls from within and without the university to "take stock of how we are doing" have been heard. While self-assessment is not a new phenomenon in higher education, much national attention has been focused on it as a result of national reports on the "state of higher education."

One of the primary approaches to evaluation in higher education is the regional accreditation process. Accreditation is a voluntary, non-governmental effort by institutions. Its basic goals are to:
- Assure the educational community, the governing board, and the public that an institution has clearly defined educational objectives and has developed an environment that supports achieving those objectives according to agreed standards.
- Encourage educational improvement by self-study and periodic evaluation by qualified professionals.

---

† *Information Technology Resources—This includes academic computing, administrative computing, and telecommunications resources (voice, data, and video). Since accrediting guidelines have been established for libraries, these guidelines do not focus on that area.*

19

The accreditation process is overseen through regional and specialized agencies (for instance, engineering and business administration) which develop accreditation guidelines and standards and administer the periodic team visits. For a general accreditation visit these can be separated by as much as ten years.

In most cases the accreditation team review is preceded by the development of an extensive self-study report by the institution that is organized around accreditation guidelines and standards. Such guidelines and standards are published by each accrediting agency. Only recently have information technology issues reached the attention of the accrediting agencies through the process of review and development of the guidelines and standards.

In order to assist with one small part of the evaluation process, both self-initiated and by accrediting agencies, we offer these guidelines for information technology resources. We avoid a prescriptive approach but rather offer a set of questions that will help institutional planners clarify their approach to providing these important resources. In addition, these guidelines will help institutional management with self-assessments that are part of the periodic accreditation process.

These guidelines were developed and approved by the Boards of CAUSE and EDUCOM, the two major national organizations dealing with information technology issues in higher education.

GENERAL REQUIREMENTS

Information technology resources, including software, data bases, computers, networks, staff, and other resources, support institutional academic programs and institutional management/operations at appropriate levels.

1. *Institutional Planning.* The institution, in its planning, recognizes the need for management and technical linkages among information resource bases (libraries, academic computing resources, administrative computing resources, telecommunications networking, and other learning resource centers).

2. *Access.* Information technology resources, in conjunction with other learning resources, are conveniently accessible to all students, faculty, and staff.

3. *Staffing.* Professional staffs with appropriate expertise are available to assist the faculty, students, and staff in making effective uses of all information technology resources.

4. *Academic Program Support.* The academic programs are supported by the appropriate information technology resources such as software, documentation, data bases, hardware, networks, etc.

5. *Management Support.* The institution's senior administration recognizes the need and supports the effective uses of information technology resources. The institution's operations and management are supported by the appropriate information technology resources, including applications software, data bases, documentation, hardware, networks, etc.

6. *Resources.* The institution's resources (staff, budget, equipment, facilities, etc.) adequately support the information technology resources and services function.

7. *Information Technology Planning.* A well developed planning process involving faculty, senior administrators, staff, and students is in place for the institution's information technology resources and services.

8. *Committees.* Appropriate structures, such as user and policy committees, exist to provide guidance for the planning of the institution's information technology resources and services.

20/ Self-Assessment for Campus Information Technology Services

GUIDELINES

The following sections provide questions to help the evaluators focus more directly on various aspects of the general requirements for information technology resources. Rather than being prescriptive, these questions highlight areas that should be explored to better understand the requirements for integrating information technology resources into the institutional mission.

Guideline #1: Quality of Applications Software and Hardware

Computing software and hardware resources are appropriate in quality, depth, and currentness to support the institution's mission through its academic program offerings and its institutional operations and management.

1.1   Are software and hardware resources appropriate in quantity and quality to meet the needs of the curriculum and research on and off campus and the needs for institutional management and operations?

1.2   Are the applications software and hardware resources regularly updated to meet the current academic and administrative program needs?

1.3   Are the acquisitions and gifts of software and hardware consistent with the academic and administrative program needs?

1.4   Are the written policies and procedures for the acquisition of software and hardware kept current and are they widely circulated among academic and administrative departments?

1.5   Do policies and procedures exist that encourage the legal and ethical uses of software by students, faculty, and administrative personnel?

1.6   If an institution relies on the computing resources of other institutions, does it have a well-conceptualized rationale specifying the roles of both on- and off-campus computing resources?

Guideline #2: Support Services

The planning and acquisition of new information technology resources are timely, and the ongoing support services (documentation, development, consultation, training, maintenance, etc.) meet the needs of the institutional users.

2.1   Are faculty and administrators provided an opportunity to contribute in the planning, selection, and evaluation of the information technology resources needed by the academic and administrative programs?

2.2   Are adequate support services (training, consultation, documentation, development, maintenance, etc.) provided to faculty, students, and administrative personnel to meet their academic and administrative program needs?

2.3   Are budget allocations for the acquisition and the ongoing operations of information technology resources services sufficient to support the academic and administrative programs, and are they consistently maintained from year to year?

Guideline #3: Availability of Resources

Software and hardware resources are readily available on campus, and where needed off campus, for use by the institution's academic community and its administrative units.

3.1   Do the operating hours of the campus computing centers and computing laboratories provide convenient access to faculty and students from both on- and off-campus locations?

3.2   Where off-campus resources are used as part of the institution's programs, are students and faculty provided convenient access to these resources?

3.3   Does a training program in the use of information technology resources exist for the benefit of students, faculty, and staff, including students in continuing education and off-campus programs?

3.4   Are there policies and procedures to ensure the integrity and security of information used by faculty, students, and administrators?

21

Guideline #4: Network Access

The telecommunications network capabilities are appropriate to provide faculty, students, and staff convenient access to information resources on and off campus.

4.1 Is there a campuswide telecommunications plan for voice, data, and video?

4.2 Is the networking access to on-campus information technology resources convenient to faculty, staff, and students?

4.3 Is there appropriate access to external information technology resources for faculty, students, and staff?

4.4 Are sufficient resources (staff, budget, equipment, and facilities) available for the support of telecommunications?

Guideline #5: Facilities

The current and planned facilities for information technology resources and services are adequate in quantity and quality.

5.1 Are the campuswide computing/telecommunications centers and computing laboratories appropriate for the academic and administrative programs and nature of the institution?

5.2 Does campus space/facilities planning incorporate the needs and standards for information technology resources and services?

Guideline #6: Institutional Uses

The institutional environment encourages faculty and staff to make appropriate and innovative uses of information technology resources to improve academic and administrative programs.

6.1 Does the institution's mission articulate the role and degree of importance information technology resources play in its academic and administrative programs?

6.2 Are policies, procedures, and incentives in place to encourage faculty to make appropriate and innovative uses of information technology resources to improve the academic program?

6.3 Are policies and procedures in place to encourage administrative staff to make appropriate and innovative uses of information technology resources to improve the operation, management, and decision making of the institution?

Development of these Guidelines

The idea for developing guidelines that might be used by accrediting agencies in evaluating information technology resources on college and university campuses was first proposed to CAUSE and EDUCOM by Robert G. Gillespie. At the time, Mr. Gillespie was Vice Provost for Computing at the University of Washington, and his idea grew out of his experiences serving on several accrediting committees for the Western Association of Schools and Colleges. He had also drafted material on computing for the revised handbook on accreditation for WASC.

The idea began to take shape with the appointment in December 1986 of two CAUSE Board members—David L. Smallen, Director of Information Technology Services and Institutional Research at Hamilton College in Clinton, New York, and Thomas W. West, Assistant Vice Chancellor for Computing and Communications Resources for The California State University System—to work on an ad-hoc basis with similarly appointed EDUCOM representatives—James Moss, Director of Computing Services at the Naval Academy, and Dr. Smallen, who represented EDUCOM as well as CAUSE because of his concurrent service on the EDUCOM Board, with Mr. Gillespie as a member at large. This joint committee worked on the guidelines for more than a year, during which time the notion was expanded to include the use of the guidelines not only for accreditation, but also for self-evaluation, which in the end emerged as a primary purpose.

When the committee had worked out an explanation of how the guidelines might be used and an explanation of the accreditation process, the final draft of the document was approved by both the EDUCOM Board of Trustees and the CAUSE Board of Directors in the spring of 1988. CAUSE and EDUCOM gratefully acknowledge the creativity and working contribution of all the above-named individuals toward making these guidelines a reality.

22/ SELF-ASSESSMENT FOR CAMPUS INFORMATION TECHNOLOGY SERVICES

BIBLIOGRAPHY

Allen, Dan. "Performance Anxiety." *Computerworld,* 15 February 1993.

"Asking the Users: How Are We Doing?" *The EDUTECH Report,* May 1991.

"Be Your Own Consultant: Review Computer Services" *The EDUTECH Report,* April 1989.

Bromley, Max L. *Departmental Self-Study: A Guide for Campus Law Enforcement Administrators.* Hartford, Conn.: International Association of Campus Law Enforcement Administrators, 1984.

CAUSE/EDUCOM Evaluation Guidelines for Institutional Information Technology Resources. Boulder, Colo.: CAUSE, 1988.

Gehl, John. "Nine Cents' Worth." *EDUCOM Review,* March/April 1993, p. 17.

Hawkins, Brian L., ed. *Organizing and Managing Information Resources on Campus.* McKinney, Texas: Academic Computing Publications, 1989.

"IT Excellence: It's Not Instant Pudding." *The EDUTECH Report,* January 1993.

McLaughlin, Gerald W., and Richard D. Howard. "Check the Quality of Your Information Support." *CAUSE/EFFECT,* Spring 1991, pp.23-27.

Meyer, N. Dean. "IS Gets a Physical." *CIO Magazine,* January 1991.

Norton, David P., and Kenneth G. Rau. *A Guide to EDP Performance Management.* Wellesley, Mass.: Q.E.D. Information Sciences, Inc., 1982.

Peters, Thomas J., and Nancy Austin. *A Passion for Excellence.* New York: Random House, 1985.

Peters, Thomas J., and Robert H. Waterman. *In Search of Excellence.* New York: Warner Books, 1982.

Robbins, Martin D., William S. Dorn, and John E. Skelton. *Who Runs the Computer? Strategies for the Management of Computers in Higher Education.* Boulder, Colo.: Westview Press, 1975.

"Ten Reasons Why Computer Centers Fail." *The EDUTECH Report,* August 1988.

"What Makes A Computer Center Great?" *The EDUTECH Report,* December 1986.

HEIRAlliance   *Evaluation Guidelines for*
Institutional Information Resources

The purpose of this document is to provide guidelines for evaluating information resources that colleges and universities can use when doing institutional self-assessments, and that regional accrediting associations can consider as part of the accrediting process. After a brief introduction, a set of general requirements and related questions, based in part upon accreditation team experiences, outline areas that need to be addressed to ensure that information resources support the mission and administration of the institution.

The term "information resources" as used in this set of guidelines encompasses information technologies (computing and voice, video, and data communications), information services, and information itself.[1] While most accrediting agencies offer standards for libraries which primarily address information in print form, these guidelines are intended to address a growing area of common concern for both libraries and information technology organizations—access to and delivery of information through computing and communications technology (electronic information resources).

These guidelines have been developed, reviewed, and endorsed by the Association of Research Libraries (ARL), CAUSE, and Educom, three key organizations encouraging and providing support for effective planning, management, and use of information resources in higher education. The three organizations conduct cooperative initiatives through the Higher Education Information Resources Alliance (HEIRAlliance).

Introduction

Institutions of higher education continue to invest heavily in information resources—information, technology, and services. The technology continues to change at a rapid rate, as evidenced by the increasing power of the desktop workstation, the emphasis on distributed computing, the use of classroom technology and video conferencing, the ubiquity of electronic servers for text, numeric, and graphic information, the need of the business community for colleges and universities to produce information-literate graduates, and the evolution of the Internet toward a national and global information infrastructure.

In this environment many opportunities arise—and in fact strong forces are already at work—to change instructional methods, research approaches, and administrative processes. Institutions of higher education need to be aware of the importance of their investment in information resources and to have means to assess their progress in providing them.

Traditional requirements for review, combined with increasing public demands for accountability in higher education, necessitate continued development of good tools for assessment. One of the primary approaches to evaluation in higher education is institutional self-study to review progress in a particular area; another is the regional accreditation process. This set of guidelines aims to facilitate and support each of these important mechanisms.

Accreditation is a voluntary, non-governmental effort by institutions. Its basic goals are to:

- assure the educational community, the governing board, and the public that an institution has clearly defined educational objectives and has developed an environment that supports achieving those objectives according to agreed standards, and

- encourage educational improvement by self-study and periodic evaluation by qualified professionals. The accreditation process is overseen through re-

[1]See Patricia Battin, "New Ways of Thinking about Financing Information Services," in Brian Hawkins (ed.), *Organizing and Managing Information Resources on Campus* (McKinney, Texas: Academic Computing Publications, Inc., 1989), pp. 369-383.

gional and specialized agencies (such as for engineering and business administration) which develop accreditation guidelines and standards and administer periodic team visits. An accreditation review is often preceded by the institution's own extensive self-study that uses accreditation guidelines and standards published by its accrediting agency. As the model for accessing and delivering information increasingly becomes one of a networked information environment, electronic infor-mation resources especially need to be addressed as a integral part of the self-study or accreditation process

Thus, we offer these guidelines in the hope of assisting the evaluation process, whether as part of the formal accreditation process or an internal institutional review Not every question will apply to every institution; what is important in the evaluation is seeking the match between the institution's stated mission and the observed environment.

General Requirements

Information resources—including such electronic resources as computer hardware and software, communications networks, databases, scholarly information in electronic form, access and delivery systems, transaction processing systems, computer applications, computer and information professionals, and other related resources—are of the quality, depth, and currentness necessary to support the institution's articulated mission, strategies, directions, and goals for academic programs and institutional management.

Information in electronic form is made available to the campus community and, where appropriate, to the local, national, and/or international networked community. Such information is selected, delivered, and managed to support the institution's academic and community service mission and administrative requirements; it includes institutional administrative and academic databases and their content, electronic scholarly information and other electronic text and images, communications between colleagues locally and elsewhere, indexing and abstracting services, bulletin boards, and access to commercial and non-commercial online resources.

What follow are some key guidelines for effective planning, management, and use of institutional information resources. Rather than being prescriptive, the questions highlight areas that should be explored to better understand the requirements for integrating information resources into the fabric of the institution.

✔ *Academic Program Support.* Academic programs are supported by appropriate electronic information resources. These comprise, for example, high-speed communications networks, computing hardware and software, access to external networked resources, elec-tronic scholarly information, library search engines and digital repositories, indexing and text and data services high-technology classrooms, electronic conferencing facilities, multimedia instructional development labs administrative databases, and the like. The institutional environment encourages faculty to make appropriate and innovative uses of electronic information resources to improve academic programs and to publish scholarly information, and encourages students to make appropriate and innovative uses of such resources to further their learning. A locus of responsibility for the institution's digital academic information has been identified.

_____ Are software, hardware, and network resources appropriate in quantity and quality to meet academic program needs?

_____ Are such resources regularly updated to meet current and emerging academic program needs?

_____ Are available scholarly information resources provided in electronic form where appropriate, and are they selected through an organized planning process, guided by written policies and procedures that include collaboration among users and library and computing professionals?

_____ Are support and training provided to help faculty and students learn to use and effectively apply such resources?

_____ Are the campuswide computing and telecommunications centers, library technological infrastructure, and computing laboratories appropriate for the academic programs and nature of the institution?

_____ Are procedures and incentives in place to encourage faculty to make appropriate and innovative use of electronic information resources to improve the academic program and publish scholarly information, and to encourage student use?

_____ Does the institution, consistent with its size and mission, utilize the national and international information infrastructure to extend educational and academic opportunities to non-local and non-traditional students? to promote faculty and student recruitment? to make appropriate information available on the network as well as accessing it elsewhere?

Administrative Support. The institution's operations and management are supported by appropriate information resources. Initiatives that make use of information resources to provide better administrative services and savings are encouraged and supported by senior administrators and information resources organizations. Information resources are viewed as having the potential to improve business processes for greater efficiency and effectiveness.

_____ Are administrative information resources provided electronically so as to increase the effectiveness and efficiency of the institution?

_____ Are access privileges to administrative information resources assigned to individuals commensurate with their scope of responsibility and need for such information to do their jobs effectively?

_____ Are software, hardware, and network resources appropriate in quantity and quality to meet the needs of institutional management and operations?

_____ Are such resources regularly updated to meet current and emerging administrative and operations needs?

_____ Are incentives and procedures in place to encourage administrators and staff to make appro-

priate and innovative uses of electronic information resources to improve the operation, management, and decision-making of the institution?

_____ Are support and training provided to help administrators and staff learn to use and effectively apply such resources?

✔ **Access.** A variety of electronic information resources, both on and off campus, is readily accessible by faculty, staff, and students so that they may accomplish their work independent of their location. Electronic information resources and provision for electronic access to information are allocated among central and distributed suppliers and users within the institution according to understood plans and procedures.

_____ Is there ready electronic access to information resources such as bulletin boards, information repositories, and colleagues on campus and elsewhere, with sufficient capacity to supply high-volume data where appropriate, and with local support for establishing such resources on campus for access by others?

_____ Does on-campus access to information technologies and services include classrooms, offices, residence halls, kiosks, and other public facilities that are convenient and appropriate to faculty, staff, students, and visitors?

_____ Is there equitable access to electronic information resources for the institutional community, with access facilities provided for those who do not have their own equipment?

_____ Is there appropriate access to external electronic information resources for faculty, students, and staff?

_____ Have the needs of persons with disabilities been taken into account in providing access to internal and external electronic information resources?

✔ **Extended Boundaries.** The institution is moving to exploit technology to extend the traditional boundaries of the campus by providing educational and research opportunities and services in the home, at the worksite, or wherever faculty and potential students may be.

_____ Do students and faculty have adequate and convenient access to electronic information resources from off-campus locations?

_____ Where off-campus electronic information resources are used as part of the institution's programs, are students and faculty provided convenient and appropriate access to these resources?

✔ **Institutionwide Planning.** The institution considers among its important information resources such organizations as libraries, academic and administrative computing support groups, telecommunications and networking services, audiovisual and multimedia facilities, printing facilities, and university presses. The institution recognizes the need for ongoing partnerships and joint planning among these groups, as well as management and technical linkages among them, so as to benefit from their synergy and to avoid duplicative effort. A well-developed planning process which is tied to the institutional budgeting process is in place for information resources, involving faculty, senior administrators, librarians, information technology professionals, students, and others as needed.

_____ Does the institution's mission and vision statement articulate the role and degree of importance information resources play in its academic and administrative programs?

_____ Is the planning for information resources incorporated into the institutionwide strategic planning process?

_____ Is there a campuswide plan for information resources that not only addresses the communication paths such as voice, video, and data communications, but addresses as well the information content that travels over these paths?

_____ Does the planning process include participation of user communities, and are users or potential

users of applications meaningfully involved whe[n] such applications are developed or reengineere[d]

_____ Are administrators responsible for informatio[n] resources management included in executive level strategic planning and direction-setting fo[r] these resources?

_____ Does campus space/facilities planning incorpo[rate] the needs and standards for electronic info[r]mation resources?

_____ Is there adequate and stable funding to suppo[rt] the institution's continuing commitments to elec[tronic] tronic information resources, including capit[al] replacement funding and annual budget alloca[tions] for upgrading and maintenance?

_____ Where information is valuable to the institutio[n] over time, are there procedures and planning fo[r] backup, migration and refreshing, technolog[y] upgrades, and long-term information integrit[y] and archiving?

_____ Are mission-critical information systems regu[larly] larly evaluated to ensure that they continue t[o] meet the changing needs of the institution, i[n] light of opportunities presented by emergin[g] technologies?

_____ Is there a plan in place to recover electroni[c] information resources in the event of a disaster?

_____ Are the acquisitions and gifts of software, hard[ware] ware, and other electronic information resource[s] consistent with articulated academic and ad[ministrative] ministrative program directions and needs?

_____ Is there institutionwide coordination of the pro[cess] cess of evaluating and acquiring emerging tech[nologies] nologies?

_____ If the institution relies on the computing re[sources] sources of other institutions or organization[s] does it have a well-conceptualized rational[e] specifying the roles of both on- and off-campu[s] computing resources?

✔ **Advisory and Policy Structure.** Appropriate user, provider, and institutional structures (e.g., advisory and policy committees) exist to provide guidance and direction in the development and use of institutional information resources. These structures are supported by the institution and are made up of members who are knowledgeable about the enabling capabilities of electronic information resources. Policies and procedures are in place to promote responsible use of such resources by individuals, by campus organizations, and by the institution.

_____ Do written policies and procedures exist regarding appropriate and authorized use of computing resources and network access, such as a rights and responsibilities statement?

_____ Do policies and procedures exist to ensure the integrity and security of information used by faculty, staff, and students?

_____ Do the institution's access and delivery systems have appropriate measures in place to assure data integrity, security, and access control, including the fulfillment of legal requirements (including copyright), regulations, and commercial agreements?

_____ Do policies and procedures exist that encourage the legal and ethical uses of electronic information resources by all members of the institutional community, and, where sanctions are applied, are principles of due process followed?

_____ Do rules and procedures regarding access and use of data strike an appropriate balance among an individual's right to privacy, the institution's imperative to operate efficiently, and, in the case of public institutions, the rights of citizens to information about their government?

_____ Are the written policies and procedures for the acquisition of hardware, software, and other electronic information resources kept current and are they widely circulated among academic and administrative departments?

_____ Are procedures for gaining or granting access to information clearly stated and consistently and equitably applied?

_____ Are information technology standards in place and are members of the campus community aware of these so that they can make an informed choice when making technology purchases?

✔ **Staffing.** Professional staff with appropriate expertise are available—both centrally and in divisional, school, or department units close to users—to support faculty, students, administrators, and staff and to maintain services. Such staff have adopted a customer-service orientation in the delivery of information services to the campus. Acquisition of new technologies is timely, and related support services (documentation, development, consultation, training, maintenance) meet the needs of institutional users.

_____ Are sufficient resources (staff, equipment, and facilities) available for network planning, operation, and ongoing support?

_____ Are there sufficient staff and funding for the identification of scholarly information resources, for their being made available, and for the assistance of students and faculty in locating and using them?

_____ Do students, faculty, and staff have adequate support services (training, consultation, documentation, development, maintenance, help systems, and so forth) to meet their academic and administrative program needs?

_____ Is there an ongoing, comprehensive training program in the use of electronic information resources for faculty, staff, and students, including those in continuing education and off-campus programs?

_____ Do training programs address differing skill levels of users, and are there strategies for providing online help and support facilities?

ARL, the Association of Research Libraries, is an organization of 119 major research libraries in the U.S. and Canada whose mission is to shape and influence forces affecting the future of research libraries in the process of scholarly communication. *202-296-2296*

CAUSE, the association for managing and using information resources in higher education, is a nonprofit association whose mission is to enhance the administration and delivery of higher education through the effective management and use of information resources. *303-449-4430*

Educom is a nonprofit consortium of leading colleges and universities seeking to transform education through the use of information technology. Its programs focus primarily on networking and integrating computing into the curriculum. *202-872-4200*

Development of these Guidelines

The Higher Education Information Resources Alliance (HEIRAlliance) is a vehicle for cooperative projects between the Association of Research Libraries, CAUSE, and Educom. In 1994, the HEIRAlliance appointed a committee to update the *CAUSE/EDUCOM Evaluation Guidelines for Institutional Information Technology Resources* (published in 1988). This committee comprised Peter Graham, Associate University Librarian, Rutgers, The State University of New Jersey; Christine Haile, Associate Vice Chancellor, Technology Services, State University of New York Central Administration; and Norma Holland, Associate Director, University Computing Services, Indiana University. Representing respectively ARL, Educom, and CAUSE, this committee made recommendations to the parent organizations which approved these new guidelines in the spring of 1995. The original document was based on the work of a committee made up of David L. Smallen, Hamilton College; Thomas W. West, The California State University System; James Moss, Naval Academy; and Robert G. Gillespie, now with Robert Gillespie Associates.

Special thanks are due to several readers, whose comments and perspectives were valuable in ensuring that the document was broadly framed to serve all types and sizes of colleges and universities: David Smallen, Hamilton College; Albert L. LeDuc, Miami-Dade Community College; and Gerald Bernbom, Indiana University.

This document was edited and prepared on behalf of the HEIRAlliance by CAUSE, 4840 Pearl East Circle, Suite 302E, Boulder, CO 80301-6114; phone 303-449-4430, e-mail *info@cause.colorado.edu.*

APPENDIX B

DATA COLLECTION FORMS

B.1: Frequency of Email Use Data Collection Sheet

Name: _____   What department are you affiliated with? _____

Week of: _____   If you are a student, what year are you? _____

Circle One: Faculty   Staff   Undergrad   Grad   Other

For each message you send or receive, please place a hash mark in the boxes which describes the purposes of the message.

Date	# Messages Sent	# Messages Received	Research	Teaching	Class Activities	Keep in Touch/Personal	Entertainment	Job Related/Professional

B.2: Campus Public Cluster Sign-In Sheet

Cluster Name: _____

Date Started: _____ Date Ending: _____

Date	Time In	Check a box to describe yourself								Check all below which describe why you are using the cluster					
		First Year	Sophomore	Junior	Senior	Graduate	Faculty	Staff	Other	Research	Teaching	Class Activities	Keep in Touch/Personal	Entertainment	Job/Professional

B.3: Network Applications and User Groups Data Collection Form

Name: _____   What department are you affiliated with? _____

Week of: _____   If you are a student, what year are you? _____

Circle One: Faculty   Staff   Undergrad   Grad   Other

What did you use the application for? Mark all which apply.

	Network application used	*Time Used (10 min. intervals)	Research	Teaching	Class Activities	Keep in Touch/Personal	Entertainment	Job Related/Professional
1								
2								
3								
4								
5								
6								
7								
8								
9								
10								
11								
12								
13								
14								

* Institutions should decide what time interval is most appropriate for them.

B.4: Online Library Catalog Measures

								Database Used *																													
								LCAT					RLIN					LIBS					INTERDISCIP.					ARTS AND HUM					SOC SCIENCE				
Date	Faculty	Staff	Undergraduate	Graduate	Other	What department are you affiliated with?	If you are a student, which class? (FR, SO, JR, SR)	Research	Teaching	Class Activities	Entertainment	Job Related/Professional	Research	Teaching	Class Activities	Entertainment	Job Related/Professional	Research	Teaching	Class Activities	Entertainment	Job Related/Professional	Research	Teaching	Class Activities	Entertainment	Job Related/Professional	Research	Teaching	Class Activities	Entertainment	Job Related/Professional	Research	Teaching	Class Activities	Entertainment	Job Related/Professional

Please mark a column for each database you use to indicate why you used it.

* Institutions should insert the names of their library databases.

B.5: Help Desk Data Collection Form

Date Begun: _____ Date Ending: _____

Question #	Date Asked (xx/xx/xx)	Time Asked (xx:xx am/pm)	Total time of help interview	Response received? (y/n)	Date response received (xx/xx/xx)	Time response received (xx:xx)	Accurate response received? (y/n)	Partially wrong answer	Wrong answer	Answered "Don't know"	Answered "Can't fix"	Answered "Can't help-manufacturer problem"	Another consultant at Help Desk	To another office within Computing Services	To another department within the University	To an off-campus help source	Please return/call back later	Very helpful	Helpful	Average	Not helpful	Rude
							Answer other than totally correct						*Referred to?					Courtesy Scale				

* Institutions should replace these office names with the appropriate names for the given institution

B.6: Network Repair and Response Time Data Collection Forms

Office: _____

Date Begun: _____

Request number	Service rep. handling request	Date of request for service	Time of request for service	Date request fulfilled	Time request fulfilled	Time required to fulfill request	Customer is? Extremely satisfied	Satisfied	Neither satisfied or dissatisfied	Dissatisfied	Extremely dissatisfied	Assistance was? Very helpful	Helpful	Average	Not helpful	Rude	Department Making Request	Address	Phone	Contact Name	Service Requested

Quality Assurance Check Back

B.7: Network Training Log

Title of Workshop	Number of Hours	Date Given	Number of Attendees	Skills Taught

APPENDIX C

INFORMATION ON SOFTWARE PRODUCTS THAT MEASURE OR COUNT NETWORK SERVICES AND APPLICATIONS

When making a decision regarding selection and use of software to assist in the measurement process described in this manual, users should consider many criteria. Some criteria common to most software packages are described below. Additional criteria for each software package are discussed under the heading for the measure which suggested the software package. The information listed below should be viewed as references to sources of more information and descriptions of what is possible, not a recommendation of any particular product or service. Please note that the various network addresses and URLs given in this section are current as of February, 1996 but may change in the future.

Solutions presented in this section for one network may not work well for other types of networks, or even similar networks at different locations. Each solution should be individually tailored to a given network environment. Users should consult their own institution's technical staff or individual vendors for the best information regarding what types of software or hardware will work best within a particular network.

Common Criteria

The following is an introductory list of key criteria that should be considered when assessing software to assist in monitoring, counting, or managing, network activities.

- Cost. Some packages are available as shareware, while other packages may cost upwards of $10,000. In house programmers or network specialists may be able to create inexpensive substitutes.

- Features. Some packages may offer more features than others, or features which are more suited to a particular situation. Some "home grown" software may not offer the extensive features of commercial packages. Institutions, however, may sometimes more easily customize "home grown" software to meet special needs and requirements.

- Ease of use. Some packages may provide an easier interface than others. It is important to choose a package that users will be comfortable using, that can be easily upgraded if needed, and that provides good support.

- Platforms supported. Some packages may only be available to run on certain operating systems. Make certain that the chosen package will run on all necessary operating systems.

- Data produced. Will the software provide the data needed to compute the various measures described earlier in the manual? In addition, the data should be reported in a readable and useable format.

Some good examples of homegrown network management software can be viewed on the Web at the following URLs (as of February, 1996). Network management staff at both sites created software to generate usage statistics for different aspects of the campus network:

- http://lurch.cit.buffalo.edu

- http://web.syr.edu/~jmwobus/statistics/index.html

SUNY Buffalo also provides a "network management" home page that lists other sources of useful information.

- http://smurfland.cit.buffalo.edu/NetMan/index.html

Other academic institutions also have similar network management software accessible via the Web. These can be identified via Web indexes such as Yahoo.

Software Support for Specific Measures

The following information may be of use when developing software that supports data collection for specific measures discussed in this manual. The information is not intended to be comprehensive, but rather to offer some ideas and suggestions that may be of use to evaluators collecting data to calculate these measures.

Network Users

Some measures described here call for development of a software program for mail servers that maintain a record of the first instance a particular email account shows activity during a sample one month period. There are a number of ways this might be accomplished.

Most commercial email packages, such as cc: Mail, provide email administration and tracking capabilities. These features allow email administrators to create log files to record pre-defined events — such as users' first logins each month.

Some email administrators may subdivide users into more manageable subgroups by category: faculty, staff, student. If this is the case, then some software may be able to take advantage of these pre-existing user classifications to analyze email usage data by user group.

The authors are currently unaware of any third party tracking software or shareware available for large Unix based mail server systems. It is possible for programmers to create scripts which will record first instances of email use each month. Unix mail server users, however, will need to consult with their own technical staff to see if the needed expertise is available.

Network Traffic Measures

Other measures described in this section call for traffic measurement on routers. Most routers already have traffic monitoring software capabilities and users should contact their router's vendor to determine what software is available to perform the desired data collection. Furthermore, many routers are simple network management protocol (SNMP) compliant — meaning that they can interact with a variety of network management software packages to regularly collect usage statistics and create reports.

Protocol analyzers or "sniffers" can be used to diagnose many network related problems by capturing and analyzing data packets moving across a network. Some protocol analyzers are software based, others require hardware and software. All vary in price and utility.

The June 1, 1995 issue of *Network Computing* magazine provides a technically oriented review of many current protocol analyzer products (Morrisey and Boardman, 1995). Readers may also want to look for more recently published product reviews.

Measurement of remote access traffic is a more complicated issue. Users of the manual should consult with their institution's technical staff to determine what kind of remote access hardware and software currently exists. Most companies which produce communications servers also offer management software designed to work with the server. Institutions should contact their modem pool's vendor to see if they offer any monitoring software.

An institution may have acquired a communications server from a vendor, or may have created a "home grown" pool of modems. If the institution has a "home grown" setup, it may be difficult to find off-the-shelf monitoring software which will be compatible with the current arrangement. In this case, the institution may have to depend on in house programming expertise to create a "home grown" software monitoring package.

The authors are unaware of any commercially available packages which will automatically dial-in to the campus network and record the outcome of the call, i.e., a successful connection or not. Users would need to contact their network support staff in order to have a "home grown" program constructed for this purpose.

Measurement of circuit activity also is a complicated matter. Several methods exist for measuring traffic on an internet circuit. Some institutions use a WAN protocol analyzer to tap into and analyze the traffic on the line. Other institutions measure the traffic from SNMP routers, which can produce regular usage statistics. Other methods may be possible.

Frequency of Email Use

See information for "Network Users" above.

Network Applications and User Groups

Commercially available software exists which will monitor users' requests for use of an application. Several companies produce this "application-metering" software. Software selection criteria should include:

- The network operating systems supported by the metering software — will it run on already existing systems?

- Extent of software monitoring desired. Some packages will record requests for use of applications on servers and on individual users' hard drives. Other packages will only record requests for applications on a server.

- Level of effort required to install software. Packages which record application usage on hard drives may or may not require installation on each users' desktop computer. Packages which record activity off a server only require installation on a server. For more information, see Boyle (1995).

- Number of different platforms supported by the institution. Some metering packages support more desktop operating systems than others. For instance, some packages will run equally well on Macs, Windows and OS/2 machines.

In addition, also keep in mind that a Unix package called TCPwrappers creates a log file of each user who "touches" the port of a unix machine. While this application will not reveal how long a user uses an application, it will reveal which users are using the application. Furthermore, mainframe computers sometimes already have applications tracking software built into their operating system software. See Boyle (1995) for more detail on this topic.

Users should consult their network support staff and consult individual vendors for more information.

Online Library Catalog Measures

Many automated library systems include monitoring and analysis functions. In addition, commercially available software exists which will monitor connections to a library system. Some packages, however, may only work with certain types of operating systems. Users will need to consult their network support staff to choose the most appropriate third party software package. Individual providers (e.g., Ameritech Library Services, http://www.ameritech.com/products/business/asg-ap-is-edu-ls.html) should be contacted directly about the support they provide for monitoring software.

CWIS

To determine the extent of use of a Web page or a gopher site, investigators can install software to count the number of "hits" on the web page or the number of files accessed on the gopher site.

- Several different types of software exist which count the "hits" on a web page. They can be categorized into three main types:

1. Software creates a graphical counter which appears as a numbered dial on the web page and keeps count of the number of times the page is accessed. For more information about this type of software, search Yahoo using the term "access counts."

2. Software keeps a log file of the IP address of each machine which accesses the web page.

A good example of this type of software in use can be found at the Syracuse University Law School Web site at http://www.law.syr.edu/stats/Nov.log.html.

This software can sometimes be configured or can track usage "threads" or the exact movements of a user through a Web site by recording each file they access, the amount of time spent at each file, the file the user entered the site on and the last file used before the user leaves the site.

Some software can also be configured to not count accesses to graphics files which automatically appear on a page. This feature can be helpful if a particular page contains a large number of images which appear by default and fill up the log file with access counts.

Yahoo provides links to a number of freeware log file analysis tools which one could use to analyze data collected from web access counting software. For more information about log file analysis tools search Yahoo using the term "log analysis tools."

3. The third type of software requires users to register by leaving their name, email address and any other desired information in order to obtain a user name and password required to access information at the site. When users return to the site, they simply enter their registered name and

are permitted to enter. This software provides all of the functionality of the first two types and allows the manager to know the name of the user behind the IP address which accesses the site.

This type of software is useful in a situation where the institution needs to know more information about who is using the site, or in situations where the institution wishes to distinguish between IP addresses used by only one person and IP addresses which are used by multiple people or large groups of people. The ability to identify the user behind the IP address allows this software to give a more accurate count of the number of different users that visit a site. Such software may raise issues of privacy and confidentiality, however. The authors are unaware of any shareware versions of this product, however many different commercial products are available.

A good example of this type of software can be seen at New Media Corporation's "Hyperstand" at http://www.newmedia.com.

Several different shareware programs are available to help gopher site administrators create reports revealing which files are accessed most often and the IP addresses of site visitors. For more information on gopher tools, see the Gopher FAQ question 33 at gopher://mudhoney.micro.umn.edu:70/00/Gopher.FAQ

Help Desk

A wide variety of commercial and shareware software is currently available to assist in documenting help desk transactions. Phil Verghis of the University of New Hampshire maintains a Help Desk List FAQ page which provides a number of excellent help desk resources including links to several lists of available software. The URL is http://shakti.unh.edu/hdeskfaq.htm.

Software packages for monitoring help desk activities vary dramatically in price, functionality and operating systems supported. Users should consult with their networking staff and contact vendors in order to find out which package would be most appropriate for the given institution.

Network Documentation Available to Users

See the above section on CWIS for information on Web page and gopher site usage tracking software.

Protocol Analyzers

Protocol analyzers or "Sniffers," can be used to diagnose many network related problems. Sniffers vary in price and utility. Some sniffers are only software-based and are subsequently less expensive. Others are hardware and software based and offer more functionality. Users should work with their network support staff and vendors to find the sniffer which will offer maximum utility at a reasonable price. A paper by Morrisey and Boardman (1995) provides an excellent, though technically oriented review of many current sniffer products.

Overview

The options available for software to support the measurement of various network services, activities, and traffic are expanding rapidly as is the technology that supports such software. Thus, users of the manual will need to work closely with their technical support services on campus and stay current with new developments that are likely to be announced in the trade literature regarding such software support.

APPENDIX D

INFORMATION TECHNOLOGY SURVEYS

There are a number of sources regarding national survey data about academic information technology. In developing this manual, the authors reviewed three such efforts: IPEDS, CAUSE ID, and NACUBO. Brief information about these follows. The data collected by these surveys is different from, but can be complementary to, the data that are obtained by the user survey described later in this section of the manual. Data from these surveys, and other similar surveys, can be useful to:

- Obtain additional information regarding academic institutions and information technology used at those institutions

- Compare or relate findings from data collection at a particular institution to national data

- Develop data collection techniques, questions, or definitions for key terms that are based on the national surveys.

The three national surveys mentioned here are not intended to be a comprehensive listing of all such surveys. They are, however, well-known and offer users of the manual additional information that may assist them in developing their own surveys.

IPEDS

Integrated Post secondary Educational Data System (IPEDS) is a system of surveys designed to collect data from all providers of postsecondary education (Broyles, 1994). It is the core postsecondary education data collection system within the Department of Education. The survey universe includes approximately 11,000 postsecondary schools divided into baccalaureate or higher degree institutions, two-year award institutions, and less than two-year institutions. Each category is further divided into public, private nonprofit, and private for-profit schools. Data are used for analyzing and reporting on trends and for policy formation.

The surveys conducted as part of the IPEDS are (1) Institutional Characteristics (annual); (2) Fall Enrollment (annual); (3) Completions (annual); (4) Salaries of Full-Time Instructional Faculty (annual); (5) Finance (annual); (6) Fall Enrollment in Occupationally Specific Programs (biennial); (7) Fall Staff (biennial); and (8) Academic Libraries (biennial).

Currently, there is little data collection specifically linked to computing and academic networks. Nonetheless, data from IPEDS can provide basic descriptive information about academic institutions which can serve as a context for other assessment data such as that identified in this manual. Those involved in ongoing assessment techniques of the networked environment may wish to familiarize themselves with components of the IPEDS, especially the surveys on institutional characteristics, finance, and academic libraries. For more information, see the Department of Education's gopher site:

gopher://gopher.ed.gov:10000/11/data/postsccl/ipeds

Or, additional information can be obtained directly from the U.S. Department of Education from contacts included in the gopher.

CAUSE

The CAUSE annual Institution Database (ID) Survey, which began in 1994, collects information from CAUSE member institutions about the campus computing environment. CAUSE is an association for managing and using information resources in higher education. The purposes of the CAUSE ID survey are to provide data for comparisons or averages, identify campuses using specific applications, and provide contact names and phone numbers.

The types of data collected in the CAUSE ID survey include: (1) general information about the institution, (2) member representative information, (3) the strategic planning process, (4) IT management, (5) IT staffing, (6) IT personnel salaries, (7) use of innovative and emerging applications and technologies, (8) financial/budget information, (9) outsourcing, (10) networking issues, (11) microcomputers and workstations, (12) policy issues, (13) academic computing (i.e., faculty use of computing for instruction), and (14) administrative applications of IT (i.e., client-server, in-house system, package name, vendor, hardware, etc.).

The CAUSE ID survey focuses on obtaining an overall picture of who manages the IT, and details about number and types of computers and systems used, whereas the user survey in this manual focuses on how IT is used by students, faculty, staff.

The Academic Computing section of the CAUSE ID survey asks nine brief questions about use such as "What percent of the faculty makes use of software in the classroom?" It is assumed that institutions will have this information readily available. The user survey described earlier in Part IV of the manual can assist institutions in gathering the information to answer CAUSE questions. For more information, contact:

CAUSE
4840 Pearl East Circle, Suite 302E

Boulder, CO 80301
phone: (303) 449-4430
fax: (303) 440-0461
email: info@cause.colorado.edu
gopher://cause-gopher.colorado.edu/
http://cause-www.colorado.edu/cause.html

Copies of the 1994 and 1995 survey are posted on the association's homepage. The annual survey is distributed to approximately 1,400 member institutions and findings are made available to member institutions via a number of mechanisms.

NACUBO

The National Association of College and University Business Officers (NACUBO) Benchmarking Project, which began in 1992 (National Association of College and University Business Officers, 1995), is a survey-based effort to create a database of comparable information about academic operational costs and service levels. The survey covers almost 40 functional areas with about 600 benchmarks. The aspect of the project most relevant here are the benchmark measures related to information technology. The survey asks for 36 different pieces of information in this area:

- Total Number of Users
- Number of Users per Total IT FTE
- Number of Custom Programming Hours per Central IT FTE
- Central IT Cost per User, Total
- Central IT Cost per User, Personnel Costs
- Central IT Cost per User, Other Operating Costs
- Central IT Cost per User, Capital Costs
- Decentralized IT Cost per User, Total
- Decentralized IT Cost per User, Personnel Costs

- Decentralized IT Cost per User, Other Operating Costs
- Decentralized IT Cost per User, Capital Costs
- Chargebacks per User
- Total IT Cost (Including Capital) per User
- % of Total IT Costs for Personnel Costs
- % of Total IT Costs for Other Operating Costs
- % of Total IT Costs for Capital Costs
- % of Central IT Cost Spent on Recurring Outsourcing Services
- Total IT Personnel Cost as a % of Total Institutional Cost
- Total IT Other Operating Cost as a % of Total Institutional Cost
- Total IT Capital Cost as a % of Total Institutional Cost
- Total IT Operating Cost as a % of Total Institutional Cost
- Number of Institutional Networks
- Networking Cost per Network Connection
- # of Users Networked When Current Architecture Plan is Implemented
- Cost of 5 year Network Architecture Plan
- Number of System Platforms Maintained
- % of Departmental PCs Maintained by Central Computing
- % of IT Costs Spent on PC Repair
- # of Service Repair Orders per Departmental PC/Workstation
- # of Departmental PCs & Workstation per Staff FTE
- # of Training Hours per User
- # of Central IT Staff Training Hours per Central IT FTE
- % of Faculty, Staff, and Students Who Are E-Mail Users
- % of Students Who Own Their Own PC
- Average % Mainframe and Minicomputer CPU Utilization
- Student Employees as a % of Total Departmental FTEs

The NACUBO survey focuses on cost data and the relationship of different IT factors to the number of users.

Because the NACUBO survey focuses on how users are served in many of the questions, it is most closely related to the user survey described in Part IV of this manual. Like the CAUSE survey, the NACUBO survey assumes that institutions will have answers readily available to its questions. The user survey in Part IV provides one approach to help answer some of the NACUBO questions (i.e., % of students who own their own PC). Also, the user survey in Part IV delves into user attitudes and elicits detailed information about how the IT is used. For more information, contact:

National Association of College and University Business Officers (NACUBO)
One Dupont Circle
Washington, DC 20036
phone: (202) 861-2500
telnet: bbs.nacubo.nche.edu
http://198.76.77.2/

The NACUBO survey provides a wealth of ideas and suggestions regarding possible measures and data collection strategies related to information technology costs and uses. There is, however, a significant cost to institutions that wish to participate in the project.

REFERENCES

Amara, Roy and Andrew J. Lipinski. (1983). *Business planning for an uncertain future: Scenarios and strategies*. Elmsford, NY: Pergamon Press.

American Council on Education. (1995). *Campus trends*. Washington, DC: American Council on Education.

Babbie, Earl. (1992). *The practice of social research* (6th ed.). Belmont, CA: Wadsworth.

Bowsher, C. (1994, May). *Improving mission performance through strategic information management and technology: Learning from leading organizations*. United States General Accounting Office, GAO/AIMD-94-115.

Boxwell, R. J. (1994). *Benchmarking for competitive advantage*. New York: McGraw-Hill.

Boyle, Padraic. (1995). Buyer's guide: Application-metering tools. *PC Magazine* (November 21, 1995): 260-261.

Broyles, Susan. (1994). *Integrated Postsecondary Education Data System (IPEDS)*. Washington, DC: National Center for Education Statistics. (ERIC Document Reproduction Service No. ED 377 250). [Note: This 24-page booklet can also be obtained by writing to: U.S. Department of Education, Office of Educational Research and Improvement, Education Information Branch, 555 New Jersey Avenue, N.W., Washington, DC 20208-5651.]

Calder, Judith. (1993). *Programme evaluation and quality: A comprehensive guide to setting up an evaluation system* (Open and Distance Learning Series). London: Kogan Page Limited.

Corporation for Public Broadcasting. (1994). *1994 Study of communications technology in higher education*. Washington, DC: Corporation for Public Broadcasting (mimeograph).

Covi, Lisa, and Kling, Rob. (1995). *Digital shift or digital drift? Dilemmas of managing digital library resources in north american universities* [Draft 2.2]. Irvine, CA: Center for Research on Information Technology and Organizations [mimeograph].

Denzin, Norman K. and Yvonna S. Lincoln, eds. (1994). *Handbook of qualitative research*. Thousand Oaks, CA: Sage.

Dillman, Don A. (1978). *Mail and telephone surveys: the total design method.* New York: John Wiley & Sons.

Doty, Philip, Bishop, Ann, and McClure, Charles R. (1992). "Evaluation of NYSERNET's new connections program," in *Networks, telecommunications, and the networked information resource revolution: Proceedings of the ASIS 1992 mid-year meeting.* Silver Spring, MD: American Society for Information Science, pp. 216-240.

Epstein, Irwin, and Tony Tripodi. (1977). *Research techniques for program planning, monitoring, and evaluation.* New York: Columbia University Press.

Fink, Arlene, ed., (1995). *The survey kit* (Vols. 1-9). Thousand Oaks, CA: Sage.

Fleit, Linda H. (1994). *Self-Assessment for campus information technology services.* Boulder, CO: CAUSE.

Franklin, Nancy; Michael Yoakam; and Ron Warren. (1995). *Distance learning: A guide to system planning and implementation.* Bloomington, IN: University of Indiana, School of Continuing Studies.

Goldman, A., & McDonald, S. (1987). *The group depth interview: Principles and practice.* Englewood Cliffs, NJ: Prentice-Hall.

Hahn, Robert. (1995). Point of View: The Keys to Wise Investments in Technology. *The Chronicle of Higher Education,* 41 (May 26, 1995): p, A44.

HEIRAlliance. (1995). *Evaluation guidelines for institutional information resources.* Boulder, CO: HEIRAlliance [also available from the CAUSE Web site, URL: http://cause-www.colorado.edu/collab/heira.html].

Hernon, Peter, and Charles R. McClure. (1986). *Unobtrusive testing and quality of reference service.* Norwood, NJ: Ablex Publishing Corporation 1986.

Heterick, Robert C. (1994). A stone soup. *Educom Review, 29*(6), p. 64.

Johnson, Sandra L., Sean C. Rush, and Coopers & Lybrand, eds. (1995). *Reinventing the University: Managing and Financing Institutions of Higher Education.* New York: John Wiley & Sons.

Krueger, R. A. (1994). *Focus groups: A practical guide for applied research.* Newbury Park, CA: Sage Publications.

Lopata, Cynthia, and Charles R. McClure. (1996). *Assessing the Academic Networked Environment: Final Report.* Syracuse, NY: Syracuse University, School of Information Studies.

McClure, Charles R. (1994). User-based data collection techniques and strategies for evaluating networked information services. *Library Trends, 42*(4): 591-607.

McClure, Charles R., and Cynthia Lopata (1995). Performance measures for the academic networked environment, in *Proceedings from the Conference in Higher Education and the NII: From Vision to Reality.* Boulder, CO: CAUSE, forthcoming.

Marshall, Catherine, and Gretchen B. Rossman. (1994). *Designing qualitative research.* Newbury Park, CA: Sage Publications.

Morgan, David L., ed. (1993). *Successful focus groups: Advancing the state of the art.* Newbury Park, CA: Sage Publications.

Morrisey, Peter, and Bruce Boardman. (1995). X-Ray your net. *Network Computing* (June 1, 1995): 62-86.

National Association of College and University Business Officers. (1995). *Benchmarking for Process Improvement in Higher Education.* Washington D.C.: National Association of College and University Business Officers.

National Information Infrastructure Advisory Council. (1995). *Common ground: Fundamental principles for the national information infrastructure.* Washington, DC: U.S. Department of Commerce, National Telecommunications and Information Administration.

Rossi, Peter H., and Howard E. Freeman. (1993). *Evaluation: A systematic approach.* Fifth edition. Beverly Hills, CA: Sage Publications.

Terplan, K. (1995). *Benchmarking for effective network management.* New York: McGraw-Hill.

Thorne, Rosemary, and Jo Bell Whitlatch. (1994). Patron online catalog success. *College & Research Libraries*, 55 (November, 1994): 479-497.

Thorpe, Mary. (1988). *Evaluating Open and Distance Learning*. London: Longman Group UK Limited.

Van House, Nancy, Weil, Beth T., & McClure, Charles R. (1990). *Measuring academic library performance: a practical approach*. Chicago: American Library Association.

Wetherbe, James. (1993). Four stage model for MIS planning concepts, techniques and implementation, in Banker, Rajiv, et. al., eds., *Strategic Information technology management: Perspetives on organizational growth and competitive advantage*. Harrisburg, PA: Idea Group Publishing,

Yin, Robert K. (1994). *Case study research: Design and methods*. Newbury Park, CA: Sage Publications.

ABOUT THE AUTHORS

Charles R. McClure <cmcclure@mailbox.syr.edu> is Distinguished Professor at the School of Information Studies, Syracuse University, where he teaches courses in U.S. government information management and policies, information resources management, library/information center management, and planning and evaluation of information services. He completed his doctorate in library and information services at Rutgers University. He has authored numerous monographs and articles, reports, and chapters on topics related to library and information center planning, evaluation, management, information resources management, networking, and government information. McClure's research activities have won a number of national awards from the American Library Association, the Association of Library and Information Science Education, and the American Society for Information Science. McClure is the associate editor *Government Information Quarterly* and was the founding editor of the journal *Internet Research: Electronic Networking Applications and Policy*. His latest book, co-edited with others, is *Federal Information Policies in the 1990's: Issues and Conflicts* (Ablex, 1996).

Cynthia Lopata <cllopata@mailbox.syr.edu> is an Assistant Professor in the School of Information Studies at Syracuse University. She teaches in the areas of library management and information technologies for libraries. She completed her doctorate in Information Studies from Drexel University. Her research interests include the impacts of information technologies on organizations, specifically the organizational structural changes that accompany the implementation of new information technologies. She is involved in the development of research methodologies relevant to the study of information technologies and organizations.